TOBEY'S 80

A Retrospective

FOREWORD BY RICHARD E. FULLER   *Introduction by Betty Bowen*

SEATTLE ART MUSEUM

UNIVERSITY OF WASHINGTON PRESS   *Seattle and London*

TOBEY'S 80: A RETROSPECTIVE was prepared as the
catalogue for an exhibition held at the Seattle Art Museum,
December 3-January 31, 1971.

"If you could sign your name to moonlight—that is the thing."

—MARK TOBEY

Foreword

A SALUTE TO MARK TOBEY ON HIS EIGHTIETH BIRTHDAY

For most of the past fifty years Seattle has shared with pride the wide acclaim that Mark has won throughout the world. Although his visits have been all too rare, we feel that he belongs to Seattle.

With pleasure we are featuring the works of the master in the Museum collection. We had hoped that through the incentive of the I.R.S. we might have increased the number to eighty to coincide with his years, but some of the especially desirable works that contribute greatly to the importance of the exhibition were available only for loan.

The Museum has been fortunate, however, in obtaining six gifts for this occasion. Two of the most notable are *Western Splendor*, which I have cherished for years and which comes as a generous gift from Mr. and Mrs. R. D. Watson of Seattle, and *Universal City*, the gift of Dan and Marian Johnson of New York City, owners of the Willard Gallery and Mark's principal dealer in this country. Miss Joanna Eckstein and Mr. and Mrs. Albert S. Kerry, members of our board, have also given fine examples, to which have been added a small painting and a lithograph from my wife and me.

Some important loans bring the exhibit up to eighty: *Parnassus* from the Virginia Wright Fund; one of Mark's finest sumi portraits, lent to us by Mrs. Jay O. Glerum, Jr.; *White Tablet*, from Mr. and Mrs. Sheffield Phelps; *Portrait of Mrs. A. H. Hooker*, lent by her daughter and son-in-law Mr. and Mrs. David E. Wagoner; *Gothic*, from Mrs. Berthe Poncy Jacobson; *Les Signes*, lent by the Francine Seders Gallery; *Dragon Rhythms*, lent by Mr. and Mrs. Richard P. Moser.

Special acknowledgment should be made of our indebtedness to the late Mrs. Thomas D. Stimson and to Mr. and Mrs. Bagley Wright, whose generosity in the past has been of great importance in building this collection. We have tried to emphasize the vast variety of Mark's talents, ranging from the family of his meticulous classic portraits that attained acclaim in New York over fifty years ago to his Market Sketches of Seattle and especially to his nonobjective paintings of recent years with their characteristic unity. We hope that the exhibition is worthy of his genius and wish him many more productive years. With affection in which many share,

RICHARD E. FULLER
President and Director
Seattle Art Museum

Acknowledgments

This unscholarly narrative of the growth of the Seattle Art Museum's Tobey collection necessarily excludes names and incidents not directly pertaining to its subject.

From those who know, admire, even love Mark—and we are many—there is such an enormous body of memory, anecdote, and other material that failure to adhere to this policy would result in an engulfment of data that would demand a very large volume.

Thanks are due to all those who so generously shared their memories relating to the paintings in the collection. Some of those who responded to requests for information are mentioned by name in the pages that follow; to their names should be added many others, among them Mr. Guy Anderson, Mrs. Ernest P. Ballard, Mr. Roger N. Christiansen, Mr. William C. Cumming, Mrs. Hollis Farwell, Mr. Harold A. Hoak, Mrs. Kathleen Huston, Mrs. Lloyd Jensen, Mr. Arthur L. Loveless, Mr. George Mantor, Mrs. Frank H. Molitor, Mrs. Ralph Nicholson, Mrs. Ambrose Patterson, Mr. Frederick Patterson, Mr. Malcolm Roberts, Mr. Guy Williams, Mrs. Theodosia Young.

The *Seattle Times*, the *Seattle Post-Intelligencer*, and all the individual photographers whose work appears in the Introduction were more than cooperative in hunting up pictures. All black-and-white photographs not otherwise credited are the work of Earl Fields, Seattle Art Museum staff photographer. All color photographs are by Johsel Namkung, senior medical science photographer at the University of Washington, except number 38, by Earl Fields, and number 77, courtesy of the Willard Gallery.

Members of the Museum staff were endlessly helpful with the often tedious tasks involved in organizing catalogue material. Among those without whose efforts it could not have been put together in the short time that was available to us are, in addition to Mr. Fields, Mr. Thomas N. Maytham, associate director; Mrs. Coe V. Malone, secretary to the president and director; Mr. Neil Meitzler, designer; Miss Miyoko Kaneta, office secretary; and Mr. Stanley W. Hess, photograph and slide library supervisor.

Mention must be made of the forbearance of my husband, John, home for the first long leave in over seven years, during which, because of the late decision to publish a catalogue, many evenings and weekends went into research and writing, and of my little cat, Yow-Yow, who felt my neglect during a prolonged and precarious recuperation.

Finally, thanks from the many thousands of us who have enjoyed the collection and will continue to enjoy it in the future to the man whose sustained enthusiasm is responsible for its size and distinction—Dr. Richard E. Fuller.

BETTY BOWEN
Seattle Art Museum

Major Exhibitions and Awards since 1958

This list supplements the one included in the Seattle Art Museum catalogue, *Mark Tobey: A Retrospective Exhibition from Northwest Collections, September 11–November 1, 1959.*

1959   Retrospective of 224 works from Seattle Art Museum and Northwest Collections

1960   Retrospective Exhibition at the Pasadena Art Museum

1961   Retrospective Exhibition of 300 works, Musée des Arts Décoratifs, Palais du Louvre, Paris (October 18–December 1)

1961   Wins top prize for painting at Carnegie International, Carnegie Institute, Pittsburgh

1961   Exhibition at Galerie Beyeler, Switzerland (May-June)

1962   Selection from Palais du Louvre exhibition shown at Whitechapel Art Gallery in London (January 31–March 4)

1962   Selection from Palais du Louvre exhibition shown at The Phillips Collection (Art Gallery), Washington, D.C. (May 6–July 6)

1962–63   Selection from Palais du Louvre exhibition shown at Museum of Modern Art, New York, The Cleveland Museum of Art, and Art Institute of Chicago

1963–65   "Tobey and the Seattle Public Market," at Museum of Modern Art, New York, and circulated in America

1964   Seattle Opera House mural installed

1964   *Mark Tobey: The World of a Market* published by the University of Washington Press, Seattle

1964   One-man exhibition at Willard Gallery, New York

1965   Exhibition of monotypes at Galerie Jeanne Bucher, Paris

1966   75th Anniversary Exhibition at Willard Gallery, New York, and Galerie Beyeler, Basel, Switzerland

1966   One-man exhibition at Stedelijk Museum, Amsterdam, and circulated to Kestner-Gesellschaft, Hannover, Germany; Künsthalle, Berne, Switzerland; Künsthalle, Düsseldorf, Germany.

1966   *Tobey* published by Henry N. Abrams, Inc., New York

1967–68   Paintings from the Collection of Joyce and Arthur Dahl at Stanford Art Gallery, Calif. (June 27–August 20), University of Nebraska Art Galleries, Lincoln (September 5–October 1), Roosevelt University, Chicago (sponsored jointly by the National Spiritual Assembly of the Bahá'ís of the United States and Roosevelt University, Council of 100 for the Arts) (October 4–25), The Art Gallery, University of California at Santa Barbara (January 4-31, 1968)

1968   One-man exhibition at Willard Gallery, New York, Hanover Gallery, London, and Galerie Jeanne Bucher, Paris

1968   Retrospective exhibition at Dallas Museum of Fine Arts (March 20–April 21)

1969   Exhibition at Peale Gallery, Pennsylvania Academy of Fine Arts, Philadelphia (January 30–March 9)

1970   Paintings from the Collection of Joyce and Arthur Dahl, at Honolulu Academy of Fine Arts (March)

1970   Graphics and paintings at Francine Seders Gallery, Seattle (August 14–September 7)

1970   *Tobey's 80: A Retrospective*, published by the Seattle Art Museum and the University of Washington Press in conjunction with exhibition at Seattle Art Museum (December 3–January 31, 1971)

Introduction

THE STORY OF A COLLECTION

When Mark Tobey arrived in Seattle in 1922—a handsome, restless stranger of thirty-two with blazing copper hair, a temperament to match, and no money—he found a small city devoid of the stimulation and intellectual excitement he had known in New York. But there were tree-lined boulevards, gardens in abundance, a relaxed atmosphere where many people felt no need to lock their doors, and a soft, diffuse light that was to become an inspiring ally.

Light, handled in his unique way as line, multiple space, and structure, ultimately enabled him to develop a new way of viewing our universe—the goal of all creative innovators. For him, as for others who have equated Seattle light with the white light of Paris, it was a beneficence that his technical legerdemain transformed into a glowing vision. Years later he wrote to a friend, "If you could sign your name to moonlight—that is the thing."

Fleeing a marital error and the increasing social demands of his life in New York, Tobey had come to a city which for years would supply him with devoted, often discerning, friendships, and an environment sympathetic enough to draw him back to it again and again. George Brown, a friend who had decided to abandon his attempt to become part of the New York theater and return to Seattle, shared with Tobey the train fare he was sent from home and

a bag of oranges, which lasted until around Billings, Montana. George also told him about the Cornish School of the arts in Seattle, and assured him that he would be able to find work there. Tobey had already known some success as a commercial and fashion artist, portrait painter, cartoonist, lampshade painter, and decorator; just before his departure from New York he had completed the apartment of Edna Woolman Chase, editor of *Vogue* magazine. He had had his first one-man exhibition, a collection of drawings, at M. Knoedler and Company in 1917. While he had scarcely begun to seek his own way, and his background was as yet insufficient to enable him to find it, he felt an inchoate desire to shatter images somehow—perhaps with light.

One of his first homes in Seattle was a room at the top of the Marne Hotel—since torn down—on the east side of Broadway, just north of Madison. Here, as he later confided, he was befriended by a fellow tenant—a woman who, sympathizing with his penniless state, used to leave breakfast for him when she went off to work. Soon he began to teach at the progressive Cornish School, where he earned eighty cents from each two-dollar fee for his classes.

Tobey's fortunes were improved through the intercession of Mrs. Edgar Ames, a friend of Miss Nellie Cornish and an energetic cultivator of the arts. Recognizing

Marne Hotel, early Seattle residence of Tobey. (Photograph by Mary Randlett)

that the articulate young man was not only a fine painter but also a first-class teacher, she formed a small class of prominent women to supplement his income. This group, including Mrs. Horton C. Force, Mrs. Stanley A. Griffiths, Miss Maude Oakes, and Miss Milnora Roberts, met at first in the room to which Tobey had moved over the Harrah Brothers Grocery on Broadway East. He tried to give the setting a certain amount of gentility by hanging a blanket to separate his bed from the rest of the room, but when one of the ladies found the atmosphere nevertheless too racy, Mrs. Ames swept them all off to her house at the Country Club on Bainbridge Island (later the home of Mr. and Mrs. Cebert Baillargeon), where they met on the veranda in the summer.

The Ameses also had a house on Capitol Hill at 1132 Harvard Avenue East, the present site of the Scottish Rites Temple. In this house Tobey painted a frieze—red and gold—in the Chinese breakfast room. In 1924, in the same room, he painted a pastel portrait of Mrs. Ames wearing a Chinese robe, which he admired so enthusiastically that Mrs. Ames laughingly asked, "Why

Mrs. John Baillargeon stands beneath an oil portrait of her mother, Mrs. Edgar Ames, painted by Tobey in 1927. (Photograph by the Seattle Times)

me? Why not just paint the robe?" The portrait was given to the Seattle Art Museum in 1967 by Mrs. John Baillargeon, Mrs. Ames's daughter, who commented recently: "This was done in the early days when Mark was establishing his true directions. He was experimenting with all sorts of techniques and styles." Mrs. Baillargeon remembers him as "a vigorous, young, enthusiastic, vital man with a marvelous sense of humor—very shy, except with people he knew best—very sensitive. He always was very individual. He would go off on his own and wander along the seashore and in the woods alone. Basically he was a very religious man; a bit esoteric, perhaps, with a great appreciation for all the arts. He never discarded those of the past."

In 1927 Tobey returned to Seattle after several years of travel in Europe and the Middle East, and the following year he and Mrs. Ames founded the Free and Creative Art School, which still exists under the auspices of the Music and Art Foundation. He continued to teach for some time. Teaching excited him, expanding his comprehension. The more he taught others to see, the better he saw for himself. In 1913 he had been unable to understand Marcel Duchamp's *Nude Descending a Staircase* when he saw it at the Armory Show. Teaching helped him to achieve his own personal revelation of Cubism, of the interpenetration of space,

and an aerial vision that amazed those who knew he had never been up in a plane. (When he did fly for the first time, he was disappointed—his imagination had transcended reality.)

The years of teaching through which Tobey learned to understand and master a great variety of painting styles as they related to the development of his own work are reflected in the drawings and paintings now in the permanent collection of the Seattle Art Museum. Tobey's association with the museum goes back to its earliest days—and indeed even before its actual founding. In 1924 he was represented by four paintings—including *Ezra Meeker* and *Song of the World*—in the Ninth Annual Exhibition sponsored by the Seattle Fine Arts Society, a group formed in 1906 to promote and cultivate the fine arts. These exhibitions evolved into the Annual Exhibitions of Northwest Artists, which were held at the Seattle Art Museum from the time it was built.

In 1928 the society held a Mardi Gras costume ball in the Spanish Ballroom of the Olympic Hotel. The motif of the decor and costumes was mechanistic art; the theme was "A Glimpse of the Year A.D. 2000." Tobey was among the artists, students, and social leaders who worked to make the ball a memorable occasion. Several of those who attended were to play important roles in the future Seattle Art Museum and in Tobey's Seattle life.

Carl Gould, president of the society, was Light the King, wearing silver, the official color of the Mardi Gras. He was designer of the original museum building. Queen was Eugenia Fuller, sister of the future founder of the museum, in a gown of silver and rainbow-colored chiffon. Mrs. Cebert Baillargeon, who was to become a member of the museum's Board of Trustees, was princess in pink satin with a silver wig. One of the queen's young attendants was Anne Gould, daughter of Carl, who with her future husband, John H. Hauberg, Jr., became a creative collector and commissioner of art works. The Haubergs made possible the building of an additional gallery for the museum, named for Carl Gould, and in 1962 they commissioned Tobey to execute a mural for the new Seattle Opera House.

Among other prominent couples at the ball were Mr. and Mrs. Thomas D. Stimson. When her husband died, Emma Stimson set up a collection of distinguished works in his name in the museum, including several paintings by Tobey. The first of these was *The Middle West*, painted in 1929, which she presented to the museum in 1942. During World War II, while the museum's director served as a major in the Army Specialist Corps, she acted in his place. She commissioned Tobey to do two portraits of

Tobey in his Mardi Gras costume, March, 1928. (Photograph by the Seattle Times)

her son, David, and throughout her lifetime remained a close, admiring friend of Tobey, concerned for his welfare. Upon her death in 1963 she bequeathed to the museum the superb portrait of Paul McCool, done in Paris in 1925.

Tobey's prizewinning Mardi Gras costume, described in the *Seattle Times* society section as "an interesting version in black and white, fantastically patterned of modern mechanistic art," is remembered by Mrs. Cebert Baillargeon, who says of him, "He was very slim and handsome, and his eyes were so shiny in those days." One of the three judges who presented him with his prize was Richard E. Fuller, who with his mother, Mrs. Eugene Fuller, was to build the Seattle Art Museum.

In 1929 Richard Fuller, who had traveled to the Orient with his family after World War I and was an enthusiastic collector of Chinese jade carvings, was elected first vice president of the society. The society became the Art Institute of Seattle after it was given quarters in the H. C. Henry House, then at 1117 Harvard Avenue North, when the Henry collection of paintings was given to the University of Washington. In 1930, the same year in which he received his Ph.D. in Geology from the University of Washington, Fuller became president of the institute, a position he continued to hold through 1934. That same year, also, his father died, and he and the late Raymond G. Wright—a member of the museum's Board of Trustees from its founding until his death in 1969—began to study the idea of a possible permanent home for the institute. As the result of a report made by Lawrence Vail Coleman, director of the American Association of Museums, Dr. Fuller and his mother promised $250,000 for a museum on condition that they be granted the site of the old rose arbor in Volunteer Park.

The new museum opened in June, 1933. It remains, with its constantly growing collections, the single most lavish gift ever made to the city of Seattle.

From the very beginning it has been the museum's policy, established by Dr. Fuller, who has served from the start as president and director without recompense, to encourage and assist the artists of the region. Thus it was most appropriate, as Dr. Fuller remembers with pleasure, that in 1934 the museum gave Tobey a one-man exhibition. There is no list of the works shown in this exhibition extant, but a 1934 Seattle newspaper clipping describes it as a retrospective of Tobey's water colors done in China and some portrait heads.

The show was reviewed by Kenneth Callahan, Seattle artist, Tobey's friend, and the adopted son of Mr. and Mrs. Force. Noting some accusations of insincerity, exhibitionism, incomprehensibility, and imitation without originality already being leveled against Tobey, Callahan wrote in his defense: "To understand and evaluate Mark Tobey's paintings does not require any mentality above the average. It is not a deep metaphysical art. It is as natural and as expressive as any art with which we are familiar." Years later Tobey said of his own work: "Some people call my paintings absolute mysteries of abstract nonsense. All things are easily explained if persons will take the trouble to see. Just as the new music of today needs a new ear, the new art needs a new eye. I can't teach most people to paint, but I *can* help them to see what I have seen. The writing style is not an abstraction. Each line has a purpose and a meaning important to the whole. And here I must emphasize it is the whole which is important. Contemporary painting is a total conception no part of which is valid without the other."

Among the early Tobey works acquired by the newly founded Seattle Art Museum were three small costume sketches and the drawing *Inca Vase* (1930), which Dr. Fuller purchased from an exhibition of Tobey's drawings and sketches held at Cornish School in 1933. The following year he purchased *Near Eastern Landscape* (1927), *Algerian Landscape* (1931), and *The Hunchback* (1930), from Harry Hartman's Book Store, and a drawing, *Two Standing Figures* (1934), from Tobey. These early acquisitions marked the beginning of a long-continuing association between Tobey and the museum, which now has one of the most extensive and comprehensive Tobey collections in the world. Museums have always attracted Tobey, providing him with concentrated draughts of visual excitement. He has been an avid collector of all manner of objects from myriad cultures—fine examples of Oriental and Northwest Coast Indian art, junk, leaves, feathers—and a trip through a dime store was sheer exhilaration for him. Having accumulated a houseful of objects, if he needed money or was planning to clear out before taking a trip, Tobey often sold them or pressed them upon friends. At least one of his objects, an African mask, wound up in the Eugene Fuller Memorial Collection of the Seattle Art Museum. It was one of a group of primitive carvings which he had bought after a successful New York exhibition,

Mask with raffia fringe, Congo, Bayaka tribe, formerly in Tobey's collection, now in the Eugene Fuller Memorial Collection, Seattle Art Museum. (Photograph by Earl Fields, Seattle Art Museum)

along with a very old Spanish wood carving of Christ.

Among the early works now in the museum collection is a figure drawing in ink and wash on wet paper. It is one of a series Tobey did while he was resident artist of the Elmhurst progressive school at Dartington Hall, Devonshire, England, a post he held from 1931 to 1938, interrupted by frequent travels. Almost none of these remain in the original, but one, dated 1932, was given to the museum in 1963 by Neil Meitzler, artist and museum designer. While few of these drawings are extant, they have not been lost altogether, for when Tobey was in Japan in 1934 he had a number of them reproduced in portfolios, each wrapped in handmade paper in which an occasional whole flower petal is visible. The published drawings do not include the one belonging to the museum. Some of Tobey's examples of fine handmade paper were lent to an arts and crafts exhibit sponsored by the Music and Art Foundation, with Mrs. Ames as chairman, and held in the Frederick and Nelson department store auditorium in October, 1934.

Throughout his life Tobey has been alarmed by hostile encroachments on humanity and on nature. At the time of the 1934 exhibition, a Seattle newspaper quoted "the revolutionary philosopher-painter" as saying, "Cities should treasure their talent and not let their artists be swallowed up in impersonal art centers like New York." Two dominant elements of mind and spirit infuse Tobey's work: humanism, based on his grass-roots American love of liberty and individuality, and the universal Bahá'í faith —a natural haven for Tobey's spirit— which accepts the prophets of all the great religions, proclaiming the equality of all mankind. One of the paintings inspired by the Bahá'í religion was a study for a mural, *Rising Orb*, painted in a San Francisco hotel room in 1935. A small, richly colored tempera painted over a base of gold radiator paint, it was given to the museum in 1961 by Captain and Mrs. John Bowen. Speaking of *Rising Orb* to a Bahá'í group in the same year, Tobey explained that the man and woman at the left represent local time, and the orb with moorings broken represents solar time. "When we wake up and see the inner horizon light rising, then we see beyond the horizon [and] break the mold of men's minds with the spirit of truth. Then there will be greater relativity than before. This light will burn away the mist of life and will become very, very great."

Tobey later painted a beautiful Bahá'í series, one of which he gave to Mrs. Griffiths to replace a portrait of her son, James Griffiths. The portrait had been commissioned and paid for, but the combustible painter was dissatisfied with it and tore it up.

Tobey's study of Chinese calligraphy, begun in Seattle in 1923 when his mentor, T'eng Kuei, was a student at the University of Washington, was continued in Shanghai in 1934 with the same teacher. This was followed by instruction in brushwork and meditation in a Zen monastery. These experiences—which, as he wrote later, intensified his own awareness of being thoroughly occidental—were crucial to his work as an artist. By the time he returned to San Francisco in 1935 he had begun to develop the calligraphic style or impulse, as he termed it—the "white writing" that was to release his genius.

The multiplicity of styles in which Tobey has painted, sometimes almost simultaneously, has puzzled and even annoyed some of his critics. As Edward B. Thomas wrote in his catalogue for the Seattle Art Museum's 1959 retrospective exhibition of Tobey's works: "The Tobey genius is not so simple that it can be easily or methodically charted. Future historians will be baffled because within a single year, a single month or a single week there are incredible variations. Picasso long has been hailed for his radical and abrupt stylistic gyrations, yet it may well be that in his own quiet way Tobey has been the greatest and most consistent innovator of visual images in our time." The artist himself had answered complaints about his many different styles in Jermayne MacAgy's catalogue of the 1951 Whitney Museum of American Art retrospective: "But what else should I do when all other factors of men are in the same condition? I thrust forward into space as science and the rest do." Light and space had become essential ingredients in his work.

Three paintings bought from Tobey by Dr. Fuller in 1936 were considered by the latter to be important signposts in the painter's development—"all very different and very important." Tobey was back in England at this time, and learning that Fuller was in London brought a number of paintings to his rooms at Claridge's. Among them were the three he purchased for the museum—*Moving Forms* (1930), *Three Birds* (1935), and *Table and Ball* (1936).

In 1938 Tobey returned to America and the museum purchased *Running Figure and Sculptured Torso* (1938). The next year he and most other Seattle painters worked for the W.P.A. Federal Arts Project. Money was an elusive commodity, and many artists, Tobey among them, bartered their work for groceries, clothing, dentistry, and other necessities. Thus it was more than the pleasure of the artistic challenge that made him welcome Mrs. John Baillargeon's request for help with her new French house on East Prospect Street overlooking Lake Washington. "When are you ever going to

do the drawing room?" asked Mr. Baillargeon. "When you give me a check," she answered. She worked on plans for the room with her interior designer, Mrs. Mabel Burrowes of Marsh and Company, San

David Playing the Harp, sketch for Tobey's original design for murals in the drawing room of the Fuller home. (Photograph by Earl Fields, Seattle Art Museum)

Francisco, but remained dissatisfied. Her husband suggested, "Why don't you ask Mr. Tobey to do the walls?" "Why, John," she replied, "that's a priceless idea!"

The original design incorporated set arrangements of musical instruments, symbols, and sketches of such subjects as David playing the harp. But when Mrs. Baillargeon proposed something less "static," Tobey devised graceful, fluid paintings composed of waves and seashells elegantly disposed in paneled sections around the room. With an appropriateness that is rare in real life, the Baillargeon house later became the home of Dr. and Mrs. Fuller, who purchased it in 1953.

The melodic flow of those murals was only occasionally employed by Tobey. He used it in *Before Form* (1929-30) and again, modified once more to a gently undulating concept, in *Modal Tides*—a painting in soft "Tobey" red, rose, and grays that received the Katherine B. Baker Award of $100 in the 1940 26th Annual Exhibit of Northwest Artists, jolting the social and artistic scene of Seattle. Two of the city's newspapers, the *Post-Intelligencer* and the *Star*, ran the picture upside down. The late humorous columnist Doug Welch wrote that to "Our Man Friday," who admittedly "can't hardly tell the difference between a blonde and a brunette until he hears them talk," the painting "looks like an air-view of a week's washing,

Dr. and Mrs. Richard E. Fuller seated before part of Tobey's mural with their late cat Coco, 1964. (Photograph by Paul V. Thomas)

still in the basket." (Welch later apologized to Tobey, who readily forgave him.) H. E. "Waterfront" Jamison, writing less good-naturedly for the *Star*, described *Modal Tides* as "resembling sun-baked mudflats when the tide is out," and mentioned the names of several more deserving (but geographically ineligible) painters whose works had not been selected.

Dr. Fuller replied to both papers with reason and restraint. To the *Star* he commented: ". . . The main difficulty lies in the fact that most active artists of the present day consider originality to be an asset. Since they often do not strive for the reproduction of nature it requires more knowledge, more observation and more imagination to evaluate it. On the contrary, however, many of the public who are casually interested in art want only the same old stuff in the same old way, for it is not easy to take. . . . My shoulders are broad, and I am glad to admit that I am responsible for the selection of the jury each year. . . . I am glad to say that I did vote for Mark Tobey's 'Modal Tides,' which you incidentally ran upside down. . . . Our purpose is to serve Seattle and the Northwest, but we would be most delinquent if we, as an art museum, did not have the courage to support the artists to the best of our ability." (Asked not long ago how he felt about the affair, Dr. Fuller said with a mild smile, "I'm very happy with *Modal Tides*. I was when I bought it." Tobey himself was amused by the furore, which served, of course, to make him better known. It is interesting to note—as a footnote to art history—that some years later, in January, 1968, Tobey somersaulted into the news again when it was discovered that his *Autumn Field* was hanging upside down outside President Lyndon B. Johnson's office in the White House. Debate on which end was up extended over a week, and finally the picture was turned around.)

In 1940 *Seated Japanese Figure*, painted in 1934, was purchased by Dr. Fuller. The following year (1941) Tobey painted one of the most famous works in the museum collection, *Forms Follow Man*, of which he wrote in a 1962 catalogue for the White-chapel Gallery, London: "When Man leaves his native place the forms which he has created follow him. They go with him and their style becomes modified in the new environment. These forms appear in the pictures, in turn being displaced and establishing themselves in the fresh surroundings." Dr. Fuller, who purchased the painting in 1950, recalls: "It was here in an exhibit, then went to Marian Willard. Then it came back here. I didn't have sense enough to buy it that first time. Then Marian Willard didn't buy it, though she should have. So I was fortunate in having a second opportunity."

Tobey won second prize for oil paintings in the 1941 Northwest Annual for *Below the Market*. The Pike Place Market, a colorful farmers' market in downtown Seattle, had always been "the heart of Seattle" to Tobey—a slice of the Kingdom of God, reflecting his Bahá'í faith in the oneness of all earth's creatures. In the early forties he spent many weeks there sketching on pads of Chinese paper his impressions of the varied scene, both human and inanimate. Fifteen of these sketches were purchased by Dr. Fuller in 1941, and Mrs. Thomas

Tobey sketching in the Seattle Pike Place Market, 1946. (Photograph by the Seattle Times)

for which Tobey created a lithograph.

In 1942 the museum gave a one-man exhibition to Tobey, who by that time had moved to a penthouse apartment and studio in the University District. Included in the exhibition, which surveyed approximately twenty years of development of Tobey's work, were two paintings that had recently been exhibited in the Museum of Modern Art, *Dancing Miners* (1927 or earlier) and *The Middle West* (1929). *Dancing Miners* is a joyous, uninhibited depiction of two bearded miners whooping it up after patronizing a Skid Road saloon. *The Middle West* was shown in a photograph printed—right side up—in the *Post-Intelligencer*, accompanying a respectful critical article by Doug Welch. From this exhibition the museum purchased *Time Off* (1941), *Still Life with Egg* (1941), *Northwest Still Life* (1941), *Still Life with White Plane* (1941), *Farmers' Market* (1941), and *Working Man* (1942).

At about this time Dr. Fuller had established a small monthly stipend for Tobey, and with credit built up in this way he acquired for the museum, also in 1942, the brilliant market painting *Rummage*, a fusion of figurative painting and "white writing" done in 1941. Another early "white writing" painting, the luminous *White Night* (1942), came to the museum in 1962 as a gift from Mrs. Berthe Poncy Jacobson, pianist and teacher. Tobey had known Mrs.

Stimson also bought a group of them. More than twenty years later, these and other privately owned paintings and sketches of the market were brought together by Edward B. Thomas, then associate director of the museum, for an exhibition entitled "Mark Tobey and the Seattle Public Market." It opened in August, 1963, attracting thousands of visitors, some of whom came from the market itself to see what the great painter had made of their habitat. The following year the exhibition was published by the University of Washington Press in a book, *Mark Tobey: The World of a Market*, issued in both a regular edition and also a special limited edition

Tobey entering the Seattle Art Museum for the preview of the exhibition of Pike Place Market sketches and paintings in August, 1963. Edward B. Thomas, left, then associate director of the Seattle Art Museum, organized the exhibition. Right, Mrs. Thomas. (Photograph by the Seattle Post-Intelligencer)

Jacobson since his early days at Cornish School, when she had recently arrived from Switzerland to teach eurhythmics. Always passionately interested in music, he telephoned his friends and her neighbors, the painters Viola and Ambrose Patterson, sometime in the early forties to ask if they thought she would be willing to teach him

piano and theory. Through years of Thursday lessons they became fast, admiring friends. Hours were spent in his studio, discussing his latest work. He would try to learn "Coco's" favorite paintings, and sometimes brought her one as a gift. In this way, through their bond of mutual appreciation and the pleasure of sharing, she came to own some of his finest work, including *White Night*.

Eskimo Idiom, painted in 1946, hung in the museum's 1948 Northwest Annual. Originally entitled *Esquimaux Idiom*, it reflects Tobey's enthusiasm for native Pacific Northwest art; one item from his own collection, a baby seal mask, somewhat abstracted, can be discerned in it. The painting was purchased for their recently completed lakeshore home in 1949 by Mr. and Mrs. Sam Rubinstein. "We liked it," Mrs. Rubinstein said, "because although it is called *Eskimo Idiom* it seemed very Northwest and Alaskan Indian to us and meant more to us than other paintings. It's a fascinating picture. We had it in our dining room for as long as we lived in that house. Some people thought perhaps it wasn't very good because it wasn't 'white writing.' But Dr. Fuller always told us if we should decide to give it to him, he would be glad to have it." The Rubinsteins presented the painting to the museum in 1969.

The forties were a most productive period

in Tobey's life. His reputation increased steadily, and so did the museum's collection of his work. Another outstanding market painting, *Point Five—Vertical*, received the museum's first prize for tempera painting in 1943 and was added to the collection. Mrs. Stimson gave the masterful *E Pluribus Unum* (1942) the same year. This painting and the "white writing" painting *Electric Night* (1944) are, along with *Form Follows Man* and *Pacific Cloud* (1950), among the most frequently loaned Tobey paintings in the museum's collection.

Tobey described *Agate World* (1945), a "white writing" painting given to the museum in 1950 through the Eunice P. Clise Fund, Seattle Foundation, in words that expressed what he was attempting with this "new convention," as Lyonel Feininger termed it: "The moving white lines symbolize the light, the unifying thought which flows across the compartments of life, and these give strength to the spirit and are constantly renewing their energies so that there can be a greater understanding of life."

Also in this period he painted *Skid Road* (1948), which was bought by Miss Joanna Eckstein, whose fine collection of Tobey's work had begun when she purchased *Pike Street* from the 1946 Northwest Annual. Miss Eckstein recalls: "It was at Carolyn Kizer's. Her mother, Mrs. Kizer, had bought one of the Skid Road characters. I was crazy

Tobey in his Brooklyn Avenue house with pupils Mrs. Ralph W. Nicholson, seated, and Mrs. F. G. Carpenter, 1945. A star pupil and close friend, Mrs. Nicholson organized the largest, longest lasting of Tobey's classes. (Photograph by the Seattle Times)

about it. So I went to Mark, having been told there were others. There was one left, and I bought it in 1948 or 1949. Dick [Dr. Fuller] had asked me for *Skid Road* for a long time, saying that it represented a series or area he didn't have. I finally gave it to him in 1961 for the Seattle World's Fair exhibition."

During this time, while Tobey was producing one masterpiece after another, he was living a life of kaleidoscopic interests,

attending theater, concerts, and movies, ailing from a series of maladies about which he complained but which he never allowed to down him. Music continued to be important to him. A piano stood to the right of the doorway in the house he rented on Brooklyn Avenue, and piles of music were everywhere. He enjoyed composing—a flute solo for the painter Windsor Utley, a work for Utley and the pianist Lockrem Johnson, performed at the University of Washington in 1950, and a suite for children were among his compositions.

Tobey in his Brooklyn Avenue house supervising Windsor Utley, left, and Lockrem Johnson as they rehearse one of his compositions, 1950. (Photograph by the Seattle Times)

When he was in town he sometimes visited the Seattle Art Museum, as he did the museums of other cities. His feeling for museums was expressed in an amusing exchange with Frank Lloyd Wright when both were participants in the Western Round Table on Modern Art held at the San Francisco Museum of Art in 1949. George Boas moderated, and the distinguished group ringing the table also included Gregory Bateson, Kenneth Burke, Marcel Duchamp, Alfred Frankenstein, Robert Goldwater, Darius Milhaud, and Andrew Ritchie. Trailing a broad-striped muffler, the architect, who was in the process of designing the Guggenheim Museum, assumed proprietary rights over the microphone, somewhat to the annoyance of the other members of the panel. "What is a museum but a morgue?" he asked. Tobey's comment, as reported in *Look* magazine, was somewhat more lofty: "Above the horizon has come the beauty of Byzantine art, the art the colored people have, the art of the Coptics and of the orient," he said. "We must have an understanding of these idioms of beauty, because they are going to be part of us." Tobey was rather amused by Wright who at the next session flung down some photographs of Tobey's work and announced, "But, of course, you are not a modern artist!"

A confirmed traveler, Tobey was begin-

Tobey beside one of the great T'ang camels at the Seattle Art Museum, probably late 1940's. He had admired the shape of the black dog lying at his feet. (Photograph by Howard Vallentyne, the Seattle Times)

ning to be uneasy in Seattle. He was always sensitive to vibrations of change in the environment, and Seattle—in fact all of America—seemed increasingly to be falling prey to technological marauders. When he left in 1950, he was quoted in the Seattle *Times* by the late Nat Lund: "This house is better suited to the operation of a hit-and-miss cleaning shop, or a drive-in boiler factory, than it is to an artist. . . . It would make an ideal rendezvous for the stone deaf. The only thing worse than moving," he continued as he wrestled with crammed pack-

ing cases destined for storage, "is staying where you are."

Throughout his career Tobey has done a number of self-portraits. One of these, painted in 1949, was given to the museum in 1952 by Mr. John L. Scott. Mr. Scott had asked Tobey to do a portrait of his daughter, Barbara, and saw the self-portrait while he was in Tobey's house on Brooklyn Avenue. When he bought it, Mr. Scott recalls, Tobey had said, "It will have to stay in the family, Scotty." But "Dick Fuller was at my house one night—we were neighbors on Federal Avenue—when I said, 'How would you like to have that picture?' . . . Dick said he would like to have it. I'm very fond of Dick —we were involved in a number of things together during the war and all, and I wanted to do something for him and for the Museum. So we got Tobey on the telephone and worked it out."

One of the first paintings purchased by Virginia Wright, a museum trustee who, with her husband Bagley Wright, has built one of the most impressive collections of contemporary art in the country, was Tobey's *Festival*, painted in 1953. Of this infectious, joyful abstraction of gaiety and lights she said recently, "It is one of those paintings that I never changed my mind about." At the request of Dr. Fuller, the Wrights presented *Festival* to the museum in 1962.

Orpheus (1952) was bought by Mr. and Mrs. Corydon Wagner after they saw it at the Willard Gallery, and given to the museum in 1955. "It has a sort of mysterious quality to it," Mrs. Wagner says. "From a distance across a room you see the figure of Orpheus playing his lyre and the sheep very clearly. When you stand very close to the painting any sense of form is lost and it becomes an abstraction of 'white writing.' That was why I was taken by it. I don't know of another painting quite like it by Tobey nor of another in which that optical achievement was made so early. Vasarely, of course, and other Op artists have done it since in different ways. I liked it so well that Mr. Wagner bought it for me."

Tobey would have appreciated her perception. Before he finished with that painting, he had made so many delicate erasures that the floor was covered with tiny rolls of paper. It seemed there could be nothing left upon which to paint so complex a plan. Often working with a brush that seemed to consist of no more than a hair or two, he could almost breathe or waft his works into being.

Three works painted in 1954 are now in the museum's collection. *Canals*, purchased the year it was painted, was one of the group of Tobey's works exhibited in the 1958 Venice Biennale when he won first prize for international painting. *Choir II* was added to the Eugene Fuller Memorial Collection in 1955. *Japanese Fantasy*, purchased in 1956, demonstrated the artist's continued use of Oriental symbols. Tobey himself, in the 1951 catalogue of the Palace of the Legion of Honor, referred to "Oriental fragments as characters which twist and turn drifting into western zones forever speaking of the unity of man's spirit."

In 1956 Dr. Fuller was asked to assemble two exhibitions for the United States Information Service, each titled "Eight American Artists" and featuring four Northwest painters—Tobey, Kenneth Callahan, Morris Graves, and Guy Anderson—and four New York sculptors—Rhys Caparn, David Hare, Seymour Lipton, and Ezio Martinelli. One was to tour the Orient, the other was to go to Europe. Mrs. William J. Lahr, museum director of education, was among the staff members who accompanied the segment that went to the Orient. Kenneth Callahan took the first part of the European tour, and Miss Joanna Eckstein, a museum trustee, took the second part as traveling curator of the exhibition, which served to introduce the work of all eight artists to an enormous international audience. The exhibitions were previewed at the Seattle Art Museum before they left the country in January, 1957. Tobey's old friends, Julia and Lyonel Feininger, wrote of his work for the catalogue: "His highly sensitive technique captures

"Three National Treasures" is the title Johsel Namkung, photographer, gave to this picture of Tobey in Japanese kimono between two men designated by the Japanese government as national treasures. Left, Manzo Nomura, Kyogen actor and Noh-Kyogen mask sculptor; right, Shoji Hamada, ceramicist. (Photograph by Johsel Namkung)

something of the fleeting values of our life; it is an expression adequate for times like ours, where old-accustomed stability has given way to changed concepts of space, where boundaries are almost nonexistent, and in which time itself has acquired new definitions; in which the intricacies of existence overlay the fundamentals of life, and man as never before has to struggle for a way out."

Tobey himself wrote that his technique

based on the calligraphic impulse made it possible to paint the rapid pace of our modern cities, but that he had now "moved to paintings termed more abstract such as *Serpentine* and *Written Stone* and a series called *Canals*. . . . Naturally one doesn't stand still if creative, and who can tell what will evolve if one continues to paint?"

The painting *Serpentine* (1955), remembered by Miss Eckstein as one of the consistent favorites on the tour, was acquired by the museum in 1958 when it returned from Europe. It was purchased with part of a Silver Anniversary Fund presented to Dr. Fuller that year at an enormous civic banquet honoring him on the twenty-fifth anniversary of the opening of the Seattle Art Museum.

Painting for Tobey has always been both a quest and an adventure. Year after year he wanders through new worlds opened by his mind and brush. Within each there is another to open after it. In 1957 he worked for months at a new collection of explosive tours de force in sumi ink. The north wall of his long, low-ceilinged studio in a University District alley was spattered with black, and so were the floor and, often, his shoes. Renewed freedom and energy were generated from these flung ink works. He wondered how New York and his dealer would accept his next exhibition—a collection in black and white. That August he wrote to Marian Willard, in a letter partly reproduced in the catalogue of his Louvre retrospective: "So for a white-writing artist I've turned into a black brush artist (sumi). Standing as I am here between East and West cultures, I sometimes get dizzy as I find I can't always make a synthesis and also that I admire both paths which should and will, I suppose, merge. My old friend, Takizaki, to whom I owe much, says that the new work is something never seen before, even in Japan, and at least has historical importance."

Tobey in the University District studio where he did his sumi paintings among many others. (Photograph by George Uchida)

Of this series of sumi, all painted in 1957, one, *Space Ritual No. 1*, was purchased by the museum in 1959. Otto Seligman, Tobey's Seattle dealer, entered a rather slight Tobey sumi in the 1957 Northwest Annual. It was rejected by the judges, who had never seen one before and did not know its author—though, since they were presumably impartial, this would probably have made no difference. Mr. Seligman was in shock when Dr. Fuller returned from a trip and learned of the incident. To soothe Mr. Seligman's consternation, Dr. Fuller visited his gallery and purchased *June Night*, a lambent nocturne painted in 1957.

An inch-long story in the *New York Times* and a brief wire story announced that Tobey had won first prize for international painting in the 1958 Venice Biennale. The Seattle Art Museum was besieged with requests for information, and the city of Seattle honored its famous adopted son on March 31, 1959, with a resolution describing him as "an artist who has drawn world artistic attention to Seattle by winning the grand prize at the Biennale." Accepting a copy of the resolution from Mayor Gordon Clinton and City Council President David Levine, Tobey appealed to them to save his beloved Pike Place Market from threatened demolition or "renovation." "If anything should happen to the market," he said, "I feel I would want to leave Seattle."

Tobey with Mrs. Berthe Poncy Jacobson, center, and Miss Miriam Terry, both of whom taught music at the University of Washington. They were attending a preview of a Tobey exhibition at the Otto Seligman Gallery. (Photograph by Johsel Namkung)

A large retrospective exhibition of 224 paintings by Tobey from Northwest collections opened September 24, 1959, at the Seattle Art Museum. Organized by Educational Director Edward B. Thomas, it included at least one painting from every year of Tobey's life since his first arrival in Seattle. So many paintings and drawings are owned in this area, many of them gifts of the artist, that another exhibition drawn from local collections could have filled the museum a second time.

It had been the intention of the museum to present more of Tobey's work during the 1962 Seattle World's Fair in a huge exhibition of his finest paintings drawn from collections throughout the world. While plans were under way, word came that Tobey was to be given a large retrospective in the Musée des Arts Décoratifs, Palais du Louvre, Paris, beginning October 18, 1961. This was an honor never before accorded to an American painter, and since it would have been impossible to borrow many of the same major works for two such closely timed exhibitions, the museum was pleased to stand aside. Instead, it was decided to mount a small but choice exhibition in the Fine Arts Pavilion. To augment the museum's collection, and fill in areas not already covered, Dr. Fuller requested gifts of four privately owned Tobeys: *Rising Orb* (1935), *White Night* (1942), *Skid Road* (1948), and *Festival* (1953). The Tobeys were installed with a small selection of superb Oriental and Middle Eastern objects from the museum's collection.

In 1960, Tobey moved to a historic fifteenth-century house with a quiet garden in Basel, Switzerland. He has continued to travel, occasionally visiting Seattle, and always continuing to work. The Seattle Art Museum's collection of his painting was augmented by a gift of two small, untitled, nonfigurative compositions, dated 1957 and 1958, from Mrs. Sydney Gerber and the late Mr. Gerber in 1965. *Garden* (1965) was added to the Eugene Fuller Memorial Collection in 1966, and *Signs and Messengers* (1967) in the following year.

The 1970 retrospective, planned by the museum as a celebration of Tobey's eightieth birthday, elicited the addition of several notable Tobeys to the museum's permanent collection, each broadening its scope.

Western Splendor (1943), a painting alight with mystical reverence, is, along with *Gothic*, one of Tobey's most famous religious paintings. The gift of Mr. and Mrs. R. D. Watson, it was given to Mrs. Watson by her parents, Mrs. Leo S. Black and the late Mr. Black, when she graduated from Vassar in 1944. After graduation, Mrs. Watson accompanied her father to the Willard Gallery in New York to see Mrs. Elizabeth Bayley Willis, who worked there. As they were about to depart, Mrs. Willis said, "You can't go without looking at my show [of Tobey paintings]." Mrs. Watson recalls, "I was intrigued and excited. I wasn't thinking about the possibility of finding a painting when we visited Betty, but I did begin to think of it then."

Bars and Flails (1944), which has also been exhibited under the title *Rails*, is the gift of Mr. and Mrs. Albert S. Kerry. Mrs. Kerry, whose husband is a museum trustee, wrote a charming piece for *Puget Soundings* in January, 1961, telling about Tobey's arrival at their home by bus with two paintings "for us to try on our walls."

"Mr. Tobey produced *Rails* from its wrapping. This picture is completely abstract. It is white against a plum red ground and is perhaps a group of weathered fence posts stacked to resemble a Chinese character. When I demurred that my husband and I had quite made up our minds that it was *The Trysting Place* that we wanted to buy, he suggested that we hang the other for a few days and added the winning comment that 'it does something for the radiator.'

"As indeed it did and has and does. This picture has through the years been variously admired, attacked, scoffed at and puzzled over." Many people have asked about the painting's "meaning," Mrs. Kerry writes, adding, "I have a feeling that if I could answer that question in a word the picture would not have held our interest through the nine years that it has been doing something for our radiator."

The subtly evocative *Untitled Calligraphic* (1953), reminiscent in shape of an oriental scroll painting, was bought by Miss Joanna Eckstein "practically before it was dry." She has now made it her anniversary present to the museum's Tobey collection.

Spring Rhythms (1961) has been given by Dr. and Mrs. Fuller from their private collection. This broken-surfaced painting in black, gray, white, and rose, lightened with glue, illustrates Tobey's use of new materials to develop his evanescent messages.

A second gift from Dr. Fuller is *Urban Renewal* (1964), one of the lithographs done by Tobey especially for the limited edition of one hundred boxed, signed copies of *Mark Tobey: The World of a Market*. It is a subject close to his heart, for he equated urban renewal projects across the land with the wanton destruction of environmental amenities for the profit of few and the miserable boredom of many. He hates and fears the "welter of overindustrialization" along with all gouging, mutilating, pillaging, and poisoning of the earth and its inhabitants of land, sea, and air. Once he wrote to a friend, "Let's hope the dirty cars are ditched and fallout fought and people stop killing each other." In an interview with Emmett Watson in the *Post-Intelligencer*, June 26, 1968, he said: "Do you know why I became involved in Seattle? It was because of the night and the clouds and the salt air. . . . Tell me, is Seattle going to become another sprawl?" Another time he wrote bitterly of the problem particularly with reference to his beloved Pike Place Market, winding up: "Oh! dear little urban renewal—what a lovely name for some sweet little girl, but let's make it Urbana Renewed." In the lithograph he pictures himself huddled in the new wasteland created by "Progress."

Universal City (1951) is the gift of Mr. and Mrs. Dan Johnson. Mrs. Johnson, who

Portrait of Tobey by Johsel Namkung

as Marian Willard of the New York Willard Gallery has been Tobey's sympathetic friend and dealer since 1944, has seen hundreds of Tobeys pass through the gallery, and she and her husband have purchased a number for themselves. Of *Universal City*, which the Johnsons sent to Seattle as a birthday offering in August, 1970, she said recently: "I don't know if it was exactly at the moment that I saw it that I bought it, but it's one we dearly love. Tobey was very happy when he learned that it's a gift. I think it is one of the most outstanding of that series of watercolors painted in 1950-51.

It is the largest of those I know of that period, and I think it is a beautiful example."

To make up the "Tobey's 80" of this exhibition, seven major works were borrowed, supplementing the museum's collection.

Gothic (1943), lent by Mrs. Berthe Poncy Jacobson, was one of the first Tobey paintings to be reproduced in color for framing, and is probably the single best known work by the artist. It has been widely exhibited, and its vaulted beauty has an immediate appeal to both laymen and experts.

Dragon Rhythms (1946), described by Edward B. Thomas as "inspired by the dances of white paper dragons in Chinese parades," is lent by Mr. and Mrs. Richard P. Moser. But they were not the first to own it. Mrs. John Tuteur, formerly Mrs. Hector Escobosa, recalled: "I bought it directly from Mark at the time he was doing my portrait about 1950. Hector didn't like it and traded it for *The Seattle Market* just when we moved to San Francisco. We only had it for about three months." Mrs. Moser adds: "I was Mark's student at the time we purchased *Dragon Rhythms*, which had belonged to the Escobosas. It was before he and Pehr cleared out everything and left for New York. We students were snapping up whatever we could."

Tobey turned to bold expressionism in painting the portrait of his early pupil,

Mrs. A. H. Hooker (1951), who herself had been painting and exhibiting in Seattle before his arrival. She, Mrs. Robert Hyde, and Miss Helen Keen formed what she describes as Tobey's second private group of women students in the area. In the summer of 1935 they met in her Tacoma studio, and later, with other women, in a class that continued to meet until World War II. The portrait is one of Tobey's most stunning portrayals, with bare patches of paper left untouched by pastel, emphasizing a vivid design. Mrs. Hooker recalls with humor that when the portrait was exhibited in the museum's 1959 retrospective she overheard someone commenting that it had probably been left unfinished because it had not been paid for. Colonel and Mrs. Hooker gave it to their daughter, Mrs. David E. Wagoner, who, with her husband, has lent it to the exhibition. "It has the elegance and whimsy of Mother," Mrs. Wagoner says of the portrait.

Most of the few figurative works among the 1957 sumi paintings are heads—all dashing and dramatic, yet each with its own separate and particular qualities. *Head*, lent by Mr. and Mrs. Jay O. Glerum, Jr., was purchased by her parents, the late Mr. and Mrs. C. Ron Johnsone. It is an almost romantic painting, with dappled, flickering darks filled with tenebrous emotion.

The antithesis of *Head* is *White Tablet*, another 1957 painting, lent by Mr. and Mrs. Sheffield Phelps. Tobey has orchestrated white in astonishing, subtle variety while working toward his mastery of light. Here is a final variation on a theme of vision and promise—a new day—presented as a gleaming field of white impasto broken by an all-over pattern of quick strokes made with the tip of a brush handle, the whole supported by a rise of red from beneath. Mr. and Mrs. Phelps had visited the Seligman Gallery a number of times to see Tobey's work. "Seligman really had about ten super Tobeys," Mrs. Phelps says. "We looked at them all and kept going back to this. We fell for it. I think that Mark really had been of two minds about selling it, and we had that nice little feeling that we may have got away with something. It's a stunning painting."

Les Signes (1962), a forceful example of Tobey's attainment of power through calligraphy, has been lent by the Francine Seders Gallery.

Parnassus (1963), which Clement Greenberg called "the finest picture by this artist I've ever seen," was the first work purchased by Mrs. Bagley Wright for the Virginia Wright Fund, established by her father, Mr. Prentice Bloedel, to obtain major art works for installation in western Washington. Most of Tobey's best work is in tempera, but he turned to oil to achieve the silent,

shifting dynamism of *Parnassus*, which was a featured painting in the Washington State Pavilion at Expo '70 in Osaka. Mrs. Wright read Greenberg's appraisal of *Parnassus* in an article in *Artforum*, April, 1968, in a review of an exhibition held in Ballbridge, a suburb of Dublin, in November, 1967. "I saw [the painting *Parnassus*] at the Willard Gallery, and I never forgot it," she says. "After reading the article I telephoned to ask if it was the same one, which it was. When the Fund was established I telephoned to see if *Parnassus* was still available—it was one of those marvelous opportunities, since it was, and I bought it this year."

The Irish exhibition in which *Parnassus* was shown was called "Rosc," Gaelic for "Poetry of Vision"—a perfect phrase, perhaps, to express Tobey's way for eighty years. In March, 1948, he had written in the magazine *Tiger's Eye:* "I want vision in my work if I am to continue. I want to look at pictures that not only arrest me, I want to look at pictures that detain me." In the thirty-two years that have followed, Tobey has painted an enormous body of work that has both arrested and detained hundreds of thousands of people all over the world. And surely some, having glimpsed the world of radiance within his paintings, have seen a signature on moonlight.

BETTY BOWEN
Seattle Art Museum

Catalogue of the Exhibition

Indicates paintings lent for this exhibition. In dimensions height precedes width.

1. PORTRAIT OF
   MRS. EDGAR AMES
   Pastel on board. 23 x 17¾ in.
   Signed lower right: Tobey. Date: 1924
   Gift of Mrs. John A. Baillargeon, 1967
   Exhibition: Dallas Museum of Fine Arts, "Mark Tobey Retrospective," 1968

2. PORTRAIT OF PAUL McCOOL
   Conté crayon on paper. 24 x 18⅜ in.
   Signed and dated lower right: Tobey '25
   Bequest of Mrs. Thomas D. Stimson, 1963
   Exhibitions: Seattle Art Museum and circulated in western America, "Mark Tobey in Northwest Collections," 1959–60; Paris, Musée des Arts Décoratifs, "Mark Tobey," 1961; London, Whitechapel Gallery, "Mark Tobey," 1962; New York, Museum of Modern Art, The Cleveland Museum of Art, and Art Institute of Chicago, "Mark Tobey," 1962–63; The Arts Club of Chicago, "Drawings 1916/1966," Dallas Museum of Fine Arts, "Mark Tobey Retrospective," 1968; Seattle, The Bon Marche, "Mark Tobey Paintings from Private Northwest Collectors," 1969

3. DANCING MINERS
   Oil on canvas. 67 x 39¼ in.
   Signed lower right: Tobey. Date: 1927 or earlier
   Collection: Gift of the artist to Dr. Richard E. Fuller
   Eugene Fuller Memorial Collection, 1942
   Exhibitions: New York, Museum of Modern Art, 1927; New York, Museum of Modern Art, "Contemporary American Painters and Sculptors," 1931–32; San Francisco, California Palace of the Legion of Honor, "Mark Tobey Retrospective," 1951; Seattle Art Museum and circulated in western America, "Mark Tobey in Northwest Collections," 1959–60; Portland, Ore., Art Museum, "Mining in Art," 1960

4. NEAR EASTERN LANDSCAPE
   Gouache on paper. 11¼ x 16⅝ in.
   Signed and dated lower right: Tobey '27
   Collection: Purchased from Harry Hartman's Book Store, Seattle
   Eugene Fuller Memorial Collection, 1934
   Exhibition: Seattle Art Museum and circulated in western America, "Mark Tobey in Northwest Collections," 1959–60

5. THE MIDDLE WEST
   Oil on canvas. 37¾ x 59¾ in.
   Signed and dated lower right: Tobey '29
   Gift of Mrs. Thomas D. Stimson, 1942
   Exhibitions: New York, Museum of Modern Art, "Contemporary American Painters and Sculptors," 1931–32; San Francisco, California Palace of the Legion of Honor and circulated in America, "Mark Tobey Retrospective," 1951; Seattle Art Museum and circulated in western America, "Mark Tobey in Northwest Collections," 1959–60; Dallas Museum of Fine Arts, "Mark Tobey Retrospective," 1968; Philadelphia, University of Pennsylvania Institute of Contemporary Art, "The Highway," 1970

6. THE HUNCHBACK
   Transparent watercolor on paper. 17½ x 15½ in.
   Signed and dated lower left: Tobey '30
   Collection: Purchased from Harry Hartman's Book Store, Seattle
   Eugene Fuller Memorial Collection, 1934
   Exhibitions: Seattle, Harry Hartman's Book Store, "Mark Tobey," 1934; Tacoma, Wash., College of Puget Sound, "Mark Tobey Drawings and Paintings," 1942

7. INCA VASE
   Pencil on paper. 16½ x 13⅛ in.
   Signed at lower right: Tobey. Date: 1930
   Collection: Purchased from the artist

   Eugene Fuller Memorial Collection, 1933
   Exhibitions: Tacoma, Wash., College of Puget Sound, "Mark Tobey Drawings and Paintings," 1942; San Francisco, California Palace of the Legion of Honor and circulated in America, "Mark Tobey Retrospective," 1951; Hartford, Conn., Wadsworth Atheneum, "Continuity and Change," 1962

8. MOVING FORMS
   Gouache on paper. 10¾ x 19½ in.
   Signed lower right: Tobey. Date: 1930
   Collection: Purchased from the artist
   Eugene Fuller Memorial Collection, 1936
   Exhibitions: Tacoma, Wash., College of Puget Sound, "Mark Tobey Drawings and Paintings," 1942; San Francisco, California Palace of the Legion of Honor and circulated in America, "Mark Tobey Retrospective," 1951; Seattle Art Museum, "Mark Tobey in Northwest Collections," 1959; Paris, Musée des Arts Décoratifs, "Mark Tobey," 1961; London, Whitechapel Gallery, "Mark Tobey," 1962; Washington, D.C., Smithsonian Institution, National Collection of Fine Arts, "Roots of Abstract Art in America 1910–1930," 1965; Spokane, Wash., Cheney Cowles Memorial Museum, "Mark Tobey Retrospective," 1968

9. ALGERIAN LANDSCAPE
   Oil on canvas. 17½ x 21⅝ in.
   Signed and dated lower left: Tobey '31
   Collection: Purchased from Harry Hartman's Book Store, Seattle
   Eugene Fuller Memorial Collection, 1934
   Exhibitions: Art Institute of Seattle, "17th Annual Exhibition of Northwest Artists," 1931; Seattle, Harry Hartman's Book Store, "Mark Tobey," 1934; Detroit Institute of Arts and circulated in Michigan, "Paintings by Northwest Artists," 1950–51; Seattle Art Museum and circulated in western America, "Mark Tobey in Northwest Collections," 1959–60; Seattle

World's Fair, Fine Arts Pavilion, "Seattle Art Museum Mark Tobey Exhibition," 1962; Dallas Museum of Fine Arts, "Mark Tobey Retrospective," 1968

10. FIGURE DRAWING
Ink and wash on paper. 7⅞ x 9⅞ in.
Signed and dated lower right: Tobey '32
Collection: Robert West
Gift of Neil Meitzler, 1963
Exhibition: Seattle Art Museum, "Mark Tobey in Northwest Collections," 1959

11–13. THREE COSTUME DESIGN SKETCHES
Black and gray watercolor. 9¾ x 7½ in.
Signed lower right: Tobey. Date: Before 1933
Collection: Purchased from the artist
Eugene Fuller Memorial Collection, 1933

14. SEATED JAPANESE FIGURE
Ink on Japanese paper. 14¾ x 11½ in.
Signed and dated lower left: Tobey '34
Collection: Purchased from the artist
Eugene Fuller Memorial Collection, 1940
Exhibitions: Seattle Art Museum and circulated in western America, "Mark Tobey in Northwest Collections," 1959–60; Seattle World's Fair, Fine Arts Pavilion, "Seattle Art Museum Mark Tobey Exhibition," 1962; Seattle Center, International Pavilion, 1963; Dallas Museum of Fine Arts, "Mark Tobey Retrospective," 1968

15. TWO STANDING FIGURES
Crayon on Japanese paper. 14⅝ x 11 in.
Signed and dated lower left: Tobey '34
Collection: Purchased from the artist
Eugene Fuller Memorial Collection, 1934

16. RISING ORB
Tempera over gold paint on cardboard. 9⅞ x 12⅞ in.
Signed and dated lower left: Tobey 1935
Gift of Captain and Mrs. John H. Bowen, 1961

Exhibitions: Seattle Art Museum and circulated in western America, "Mark Tobey in Northwest Collections," 1959–60; Seattle World's Fair, Fine Arts Pavilion, "Seattle Art Museum Mark Tobey Exhibition," 1962

17. THREE BIRDS
Gouache on paper. 10¾ x 14⅞ in.
Signed and dated lower right: Tobey '35
Collection: Purchased from the artist
Eugene Fuller Memorial Collection, 1936
Exhibitions: Tacoma, Wash., College of Puget Sound, "Mark Tobey Drawings and Paintings," 1942; San Francisco, California Palace of the Legion of Honor and circulated in America, "Mark Tobey Retrospective," 1951; Seattle Art Museum and circulated in western America, "Mark Tobey in Northwest Collections," 1959–60; Paris, Musée des Arts Décoratifs, "Mark Tobey," 1961; New York, Museum of Modern Art, The Cleveland Museum of Art, and Art Institute of Chicago, "Mark Tobey," 1962–63; University of Arizona Art Gallery, "The Bird in Art," 1964; Spokane, Wash., Cheney Cowles Memorial Museum, "Mark Tobey Retrospective," 1968; Halifax, Canada, Nova Scotia Museum of Fine Arts, "Painters of the Northwest School," 1969

18. TABLE AND BALL
Gouache on paper. 10½ x 19½ in.
Signed and dated lower right: Tobey '36'
Collection: Purchased from the artist
Eugene Fuller Memorial Collection, 1936
Exhibitions: San Francisco, California Palace of the Legion of Honor and circulated in America, "Mark Tobey Retrospective," 1951; Seattle Art Museum, "Mark Tobey in Northwest Collections," 1959; Paris, Musée des Arts Décoratifs, "Mark Tobey," 1961; New York, Museum of Modern Art, The Cleveland Museum of Art, and Art Institute of Chicago, "Mark Tobey," 1962–

63; Spokane, Wash., Cheney Cowles Memorial Museum, "Mark Tobey Retrospective," 1968

19. RUNNING FIGURE AND SCULPTURED TORSO
Pen and ink on paper. 15 x 20 in.
Signed and dated lower right: Tobey 1938
Collection: Purchased from the artist
Eugene Fuller Memorial Collection, 1938

20. MODAL TIDE
Oil on canvas. 34½ x 47⅜ in.
Signed and dated lower right: Tobey '40
Katherine B. Baker Memorial Purchase Prize, 26th Northwest Annual, 1940
Exhibitions: Seattle Art Museum, "26th Annual Exhibition of Northwest Artists," 1940; San Francisco, California Palace of the Legion of Honor and circulated in America, "Mark Tobey Retrospective," 1951; Seattle Art Museum and circulated in western America, "Mark Tobey in Northwest Collections," 1959–60; Anchorage, Alaska Methodist University, "Twenty-five Years of Award Paintings," 1960; Seattle World's Fair, Fine Arts Pavilion, "Seattle Art Museum Mark Tobey Exhibition," 1962; Pittsburgh, Carnegie Institute, Museum of Art, "The Seashore: Paintings of the 19th and 20th Centuries," 1965; Spokane, Wash., Cheney Cowles Memorial Museum, "Mark Tobey Retrospective," 1968; Seattle, The Bon Marche, "Mark Tobey Paintings from Private Northwest Collectors," 1969

21. FARMERS' MARKET
Gouache on board. 19⅝ x 15⅝ in.
Signed and dated lower left: Tobey 41
Eugene Fuller Memorial Collection, 1942
Exhibitions: Seattle Art Museum, "Mark Tobey," 1942; University of Oklahoma, "Northwest Artists," 1946; Washington, D.C., United States Information Agency for circulation in Europe, "25 Years of American Painting," 1959–60;

Seattle World's Fair, Fine Arts Pavilion, "Seattle Art Museum Mark Tobey Exhibition," 1962; Dallas Museum of Fine Arts, "Mark Tobey Retrospective," 1968; The Cleveland Institute of Art, "A View of Contemporary American Watercolor," 1968

22. **NORTHWEST STILL LIFE**
Tempera on board. 20 x 26 in.
Signed and dated lower right: Tobey '41
Eugene Fuller Memorial Collection, 1942
Exhibitions: Seattle Art Museum, "Mark Tobey," 1942; Portland, Ore. Art Museum, San Francisco Museum of Art, and Detroit Institute of Arts, "Paintings by Mark Tobey," 1945–46; Detroit Institute of Arts and circulated in Michigan, "Paintings by Northwest Artists," 1950–51; Dallas Museum of Fine Arts, "Mark Tobey Retrospective," 1968

23–37. **15 PUBLIC MARKET TYPES**
Pen and tempera on paper. 8⅝ x 5⅝ in.
Signed and dated lower right: Tobey 41
Collection: Purchased from the artist
Eugene Fuller Memorial Collection, 1941
Exhibitions: Seattle World's Fair, Fine Arts Pavilion, "Seattle Art Museum Mark Tobey Exhibition," 1962; New York, Museum of Modern Art and circulated in America, "Tobey and the Seattle Public Market," 1963–65

38. **RUMMAGE**
Gouache on fiberboard. 38⅜ x 25⅞ in.
Signed and dated lower right: Tobey 41
Eugene Fuller Memorial Collection, 1942
Exhibitions: Seattle Art Museum, "Mark Tobey," 1942; Tacoma, Wash., College of Puget Sound, "Mark Tobey Drawings and Paintings," 1942; New York, Museum of Modern Art and circuit, "Fourteen Americans," 1946; Detroit Institute of Arts and circulated in Michigan, "Paintings by Northwest Artists," 1950–51; Washington, D.C., United States Information Agency for

circulation in Europe, "Eight American Artists," 1957–58; Seattle Art Museum and circulated in western America, "Mark Tobey in Northwest Collections," 1959–60; Milwaukee Art Center, "Ten Americans," 1961; Seattle World's Fair, Fine Arts Pavilion, "Seattle Art Museum Mark Tobey Exhibition," 1962; Fort Worth, Tex., Amon Carter Museum, Los Angeles, University of California Art Gallery, and Oakland Art Museum, "Artist's Environment; West Coast," 1962–63; New York, Museum of Modern Art and circulated in America, "Tobey and the Seattle Public Market," 1963–65; Dallas Museum of Fine Arts, "Mark Tobey Retrospective," 1968; Seattle, The Bon Marche, "Mark Tobey Paintings from Private Northwest Collectors," 1969; Osaka, Japan, Expo '70, Expo Museum of Fine Arts, "International Fine Arts Exhibition," 1970

39. **STILL LIFE WITH EGG**
Tempera. 10⅝ x 17 in.
Signed and dated lower right: Tobey 41
Eugene Fuller Memorial Collection, 1942
Exhibitions: Seattle Art Museum, "Mark Tobey," 1942; Tacoma, Wash., College of Puget Sound, "Mark Tobey Drawings and Paintings," 1942; Seattle Art Museum and circulated in western America, "Mark Tobey in Northwest Collections," 1959–60; Seattle World's Fair, Fine Arts Pavilion, "Seattle Art Museum Mark Tobey Exhibition," 1962

40. **STILL LIFE WITH WHITE PLANE**
Gouache on board. 17⅝ x 21¾ in.
Signed and dated lower left: Tobey 41
Eugene Fuller Memorial Collection, 1942
Exhibitions: Seattle Art Museum, "Mark Tobey," 1942; Tacoma, Wash., College of Puget Sound, "Mark Tobey Drawings and Paintings," 1942; Seattle, Western Association of Art Museums for circulation, "Pacific Coast Painters," 1947; San Francisco, California Palace of the Legion of

Honor and circulated in America, "Mark Tobey Retrospective," 1951; Seattle Art Museum and circulated in western America, "Mark Tobey in Northwest Collections," 1959–60; Seattle World's Fair, Fine Arts Pavilion, "Seattle Art Museum Mark Tobey Exhibition," 1962; Spokane, Wash., Cheney Cowles Memorial Museum, "Mark Tobey Retrospective," 1968

41. **TIME OFF**
Oil on board. 19⅝ x 15½ in.
Signed and dated lower left: Tobey '41
Eugene Fuller Memorial Collection, 1942
Exhibitions: Seattle Art Museum, "Mark Tobey," 1942; Tacoma, Wash., College of Puget Sound, "Mark Tobey Drawings and Paintings," 1942; Portland, Ore., Art Museum, San Francisco Museum of Art, and Detroit Institute of Arts, "Paintings by Mark Tobey," 1945; Seattle Art Museum and circulated in western America, "Mark Tobey in Northwest Collections," 1959–60; Seattle World's Fair, Fine Arts Pavilion, Seattle Art Museum Mark Tobey Exhibition," 1962; Dallas Museum of Fine Arts, "Mark Tobey Retrospective," 1968

42. **FORMS FOLLOW MAN**
Gouache on cardboard. 13⅝ x 19⅝ in.
Date: 1941.
Signed and dated lower right: Tobey '43
Collection: Purchased from the artist
Eugene Fuller Memorial Collection, 1950
Exhibitions: Seattle Art Museum, "27th Annual Exhibition of Northwest Artists," 1941; Portland, Ore., Art Museum, San Francisco Museum of Art, and Detroit Institute of Arts, "Paintings by Mark Tobey," 1945–46; Detroit Institute of Arts and circulated in Michigan, "Paintings by Northwest Artists," 1950–51; The Art Institute of Chicago, "Tobey Retrospective," 1955; San Francisco Museum of Art, United Nations Exhibition, "Art in the 20th Century," 1955; Washington, D.C., United States Information

Agency for circulation in Asia and Australia, "Eight American Artists," 1957–58; Seattle Art Museum and circulated in western America, "Mark Tobey in Northwest Collections," 1959–60; Paris, Musée des Arts Décoratifs, "Mark Tobey," 1961; London, Whitechapel Gallery, "Mark Tobey," 1962; New York, Museum of Modern Art, The Cleveland Museum of Art, and Art Institute of Chicago, "Mark Tobey," 1962–63; Amsterdam, Stedelijk Museum and circulated in Europe, "Mark Tobey," 1966; Dallas Museum of Fine Arts, "Mark Tobey Retrospective," 1968; Seattle, The Bon Marche, "Mark Tobey Paintings from Private Northwest Collectors," 1969

43. E PLURIBUS UNUM
Tempera on paper mounted on board. 19¾ x 27¼ in.
Signed and dated upper right: Tobey '42
Collection: Willard Gallery, New York
Gift of Mrs. Thomas D. Stimson, 1943
Exhibitions: New York, Willard Gallery, "Mark Tobey," 1944; Portland, Ore., Art Museum, San Francisco Museum of Art, and Detroit Institute of Arts, "Paintings by Mark Tobey," 1945–46; New York, Museum of Modern Art and circuit, "Fourteen Americans," 1946; New York, Munson-Williams-Proctor Institute and circulated in eastern America, "Ten Northwest Painters," 1947–48; Seattle, Western Association of Art Museums for circulation on the West Coast and in British Columbia, "Trio," 1950–51; San Francisco, California Palace of the Legion of Honor and circulated in America, "Mark Tobey Retrospective," 1951; Art Institute of Chicago, "Tobey Retrospective," 1955; Seattle Art Museum and circulated in western America, "Mark Tobey in Northwest Collections," 1959–60; Paris, Musée des Arts Décoratifs, "Mark Tobey," 1961; London, Whitechapel Gallery, "Mark Tobey," 1962; Washington, D.C., The Phillips

Collection, "Mark Tobey Exhibition," 1962; New York, Museum of Modern Art, Cleveland Museum of Art, and Art Institute of Chicago, "Mark Tobey," 1962–63; Amsterdam, Stedelijk Museum and circulated in Europe, "Mark Tobey," 1966; Spokane, Wash., Cheney Cowles Memorial Museum, "Mark Tobey Retrospective," 1968; The Arts Club of Chicago, "The Crowd," 1969

44. WHITE NIGHT
Tempera on cardboard mounted on masonite. 22¼ x 14 in.
Signed and dated lower right: Tobey 42
Gift of Mrs. Berthe Poncy Jacobson, 1962
Exhibitions: Portland, Ore., Art Museum, San Francisco Museum of Art, and Detroit Institute of Arts, "Paintings by Mark Tobey," 1945–46; San Francisco, California Palace of the Legion of Honor and circulated in America, "Mark Tobey Retrospective," 1951; Seattle Art Museum and circulated in western America, "Mark Tobey in Northwest Collections," 1959–60; Seattle World's Fair, Fine Arts Pavilion, "Seattle Art Museum Mark Tobey Exhibition," 1962; Spokane, Wash., Cheney Cowles Memorial Museum, "Mark Tobey Retrospective," 1968; Seattle, The Bon Marche, "Mark Tobey Paintings from Private Northwest Collectors," 1969

45. WORKING MAN
Gouache on board. 43½ x 27½ in.
Signed and dated lower right: Tobey '42
Eugene Fuller Memorial Collection, 1942
Exhibitions: Seattle, Western Association of Art Museums for circulation, "Pacific Coast Painters," 1947; San Francisco, California Palace of the Legion of Honor and circulated in America, "Mark Tobey Retrospective," 1951; Seattle Art Museum and circulated in western America, "Mark Tobey in Northwest Collections," 1959–60; Seattle World's Fair, Fine Arts Pavilion, "Seattle Art Museum Mark Tobey Exhibition,"

1962; Seattle, University of Washington, Henry Gallery, "Figure Painting Exhibition," 1962

46. GOTHIC*
Tempera. 27¾ x 21⅛ in.
Unsigned. Date: 1943
Lent by Mrs. Berthe Poncy Jacobson, Seattle, 1970
Exhibitions: San Francisco, California Palace of the Legion of Honor, "Mark Tobey Retrospective," 1951; Seattle Art Museum and circulated in western America, "Mark Tobey in Northwest Collections," 1959–60; Paris, Musée des Arts Décoratifs, "Mark Tobey," 1961; London, Whitechapel Gallery, "Mark Tobey," 1962; New York, Museum of Modern Art, The Cleveland Museum of Art, and Art Institute of Chicago, "Mark Tobey," 1962–63; Amsterdam, Stedelijk Museum and circulated in Europe, "Mark Tobey," 1966; Dallas Museum of Fine Arts, "Mark Tobey Retrospective," 1968

47. POINT FIVE—VERTICAL
Gouache on board. 28½ x 19⅛ in.
Signed and dated lower right: Tobey 43
Seattle Art Museum Purchase Prize, 29th Annual Exhibition of Northwest Artists, 1943
Exhibitions: Seattle Art Museum, "29th Annual Exhibition of Northwest Artists," 1943; Portland, Ore., Art Museum, San Francisco Museum of Art, and Detroit Institute of Arts, "Paintings by Mark Tobey," 1945–46; Detroit Institute of Arts and circulated in Michigan, "Paintings by Northwest Artists," 1950–51; Seattle Art Museum, "Mark Tobey in Northwest Collections," 1959; Seattle World's Fair, Fine Arts Pavilion, "Seattle Art Museum Mark Tobey Exhibition," 1962; Dallas Museum of Fine Arts, "Mark Tobey Retrospective," 1968

48. WESTERN SPLENDOR
Tempera. 25¾ x 19¼ in.
Signed and dated lower right: Tobey 43

Collection: Willard Gallery, New York
Gift of Mr. and Mrs. R. D. Watson, 1970
Exhibitions: New York, Willard Gallery, "Mark Tobey," 1944; Washington, D.C., United States Information Agency for circulation in Europe, "Eight American Artists," 1957–58; Seattle Art Museum, "Mark Tobey in Northwest Collections," 1959; Washington, D.C., Gallery of Modern Art, and Seattle Art Museum, in collaboration with Contemporary Art Council (Seattle Art Museum), "Twentieth Century Painting from Collections in the State of Washington," 1966; Seattle, The Bon Marche, "Mark Tobey Paintings from Private Northwest Collectors," 1969

49. BARS AND FLAILS (RAILS)
Tempera. 21½ x 15⅝ in.
Signed and dated lower left: Tobey 44
Collection: Purchased from the artist
Gift of Mr. and Mrs. A. S. Kerry, 1970
Exhibitions: Seattle, "35th Annual Exhibition of Northwest Artists," 1949; Seattle, The Bon Marche, "Mark Tobey Paintings from Private Northwest Collectors," 1969

50. ELECTRIC NIGHT
Tempera on paper mounted on board. 17½ x 13 in.
Signed and dated lower right: Tobey 44
Collection: Purchased from the artist
Eugene Fuller Memorial Collection, 1944
Exhibitions: New York, Willard Gallery, "Mark Tobey," 1944; Portland, Ore., Art Museum, San Francisco Museum of Art, and Detroit Institute of Arts, "Paintings by Mark Tobey," 1945–46; New York, Museum of Modern Art, "Fourteen Americans," 1946; San Francisco Museum of Art, "Special Exhibition in conjunction with the Western Round Table on Modern Art," 1949; Seattle, Western Association of Art Museums for circulation on the West Coast and in

British Columbia, "Trio," 1950-51; San Francisco, California Palace of the Legion of Honor and circulated in America, "Mark Tobey Retrospective," 1951; Houston, Tex., Contemporary Arts Association, "Marin, Tobey, Graves," 1956; New York, The American Federation of Arts for United States Information Agency circulation in Europe, "American Painting 1900-55," 1956; Washington, D.C., United States Information Agency for circulation in Europe, "Eight American Artists," 1957-58; Seattle Art Museum and circulated in western America, "Mark Tobey in Northwest Collections," 1959-60; Paris, Musée des Arts Décoratifs, "Mark Tobey," 1961; London, Whitechapel Gallery, "Mark Tobey," 1962; New York, Museum of Modern Art, The Cleveland Museum of Art, and Art Institute of Chicago, "Mark Tobey," 1962-63; The Arts Club of Chicago, "The Crowd," 1969

51. AGATE WORLD
Gouache on board. 14⅞ x 11 in.
Signed and dated lower left: Tobey 45
Collection: Purchased from the artist
Gift of Eunice P. Clise Fund, Seattle Foundation, 1950
Exhibitions: San Francisco, California Palace of the Legion of Honor and circulated in America, "Mark Tobey Retrospective," 1951; Houston, Tex., Contemporary Arts Association, "Marin, Tobey, Graves," 1956; Pennsylvania, University of Pittsburgh, "Calligraphy: The Symbolic Line in the Art of Writing and in the Arts of Form," 1957; San Francisco Museum of Art, "Art in Asia and the West," 1957; Seattle Art Museum and circulated in western America, "Mark Tobey in Northwest Collections," 1959-60; Paris, Musée des Arts Décoratifs, "Mark Tobey," 1961; London, Whitechapel Gallery, "Mark Tobey," 1962; New York, Museum of Modern Art, The Cleveland Museum of Art, and Art Institute of Chicago, "Mark Tobey," 1962-63; Dallas Mu-

seum of Fine Arts, "Mark Tobey Retrospective," 1968; Tacoma, Wash., University of Puget Sound, "Northwest Art," 1969

52. DRAGON RHYTHMS*
Tempera. 18¼ x 24½ in.
Signed and dated lower right: Tobey '46
Collection: Mr. and Mrs. Hector Escobosa
Lent by Mr. and Mrs. Richard P. Moser, California, 1970
Exhibitions: Seattle Art Museum and circulated in western America, "Mark Tobey in Northwest Collections," 1959-60; Paris, Musée des Arts Décoratifs, "Mark Tobey," 1961

53. ESKIMO IDIOM
Tempera on board. 43½ x 27½ in.
Unsigned. Date: 1946
Gift of Mr. and Mrs. Sam Rubinstein, 1969
Exhibitions: Seattle Art Museum, "34th Annual Exhibition of Northwest Artists," 1948; San Francisco, California Palace of the Legion of Honor and circulated in America, "Mark Tobey Retrospective," 1951; Seattle Art Museum and circulated in western America, "Mark Tobey in Northwest Collections," 1959-60; Paris, Musée des Arts Décoratifs, "Mark Tobey," 1961; New York, Museum of Modern Art, The Cleveland Museum of Art, and Art Institute of Chicago, "Mark Tobey," 1962-63; Washington, D.C., Gallery of Modern Art and Seattle Art Museum, in collaboration with Contemporary Art Council (Seattle Art Museum), "Twentieth Century Painting from Collections in the State of Washington," 1966

54. SKID ROAD
Watercolor. 24⅝ x 18½ in.
Signed and dated: Tobey 48
Gift of Miss Joanna Eckstein, 1961
Exhibition: Seattle World's Fair, Fine Arts Pavilion, "Seattle Art Museum Mark Tobey Exibition," 1962

55. SELF PORTRAIT
Pastel on paper. 20½ x 12 in.
Signed and dated on back: Tobey '49
Collection: Purchased from the artist
Gift of John L. Scott, 1952
Exhibitions: California, Stanford University, "20th Century Drawings," 1955; Seattle Art Museum and circulated in western America, "Mark Tobey in Northwest Collections," 1959–60; Seattle World's Fair, Fine Arts Pavilion, "Seattle Art Museum Mark Tobey Exhibition," 1962; Dallas Museum of Fine Arts, "Mark Tobey Retrospective," 1968; Seattle, The Bon Marche, "Mark Tobey Paintings from Private Northwest Collectors," 1969

56. MOUNTAIN LANDSCAPE
Gouache on paper. 14½ x 16 in.
Signed and dated lower right: Tobey 50
Collection: Purchased from the artist
Eugene Fuller Memorial Collection, 1951
Exhibitions: San Francisco, Palace of the Legion of Honor and circulated in America, "Mark Tobey Retrospective," 1951; San Francisco Museum of Art, "Art in Asia and the West," 1957; Seattle Art Museum and circulated in western America, "Mark Tobey in Northwest Collections," 1959–60; Paris, Musée des Arts Décoratifs, "Mark Tobey," 1961; Minneapolis Institute of Arts, "Four Centuries of American Art," 1964; Spokane, Wash., Cheney Cowles Memorial Museum, "Mark Tobey Retrospective," 1968

57. PACIFIC CLOUD
Gouache on paper. 12⅞ x 18¼ in.
Signed and dated lower right: Tobey 50
Collection: Purchased from the artist
Eugene Fuller Memorial Collection, 1951
Exhibitions: San Francisco, California Palace of the Legion of Honor and circulated in America, "Mark Tobey Retrospective," 1951; Colorado Springs Fine Arts Center, "New Accessions

U.S.A.," 1952; Houston, Tex., Contemporary Arts Association, "Marin, Tobey, Graves," 1956; Sacramento, California State Fair, 1956; New York, The American Federation of Arts for circulation in eastern America, "Cross-currents," 1958–59; New York, The American Federation of Arts for circulation in eastern American, "Private Worlds," 1960–61; Paris, Musée des Arts Décoratifs, "Mark Tobey," 1961; London, Whitechapel Gallery, "Mark Tobey," 1962; New York, Museum of Modern Art, The Cleveland Museum of Art, and Art Institute of Chicago, "Mark Tobey," 1962–63; Spokane, Wash., Cheney Cowles Memorial Museum, "Mark Tobey Retrospective," 1968

58. UNIVERSAL CITY
Watercolor. 37½ x 25 in.
Unsigned. Date: 1951
Gift of Mr. and Mrs. Dan Johnson, New York, 1970
Exhibitions: New York, The American Federation of Arts, "American Vanguards for Paris," 1953; New York, National Institute of Arts and Letters, 1956; Washington, D.C., St. Albans University, "Mark Tobey," 1956; New York, World House Gallery, 1957; New York, Museum of Modern Art, The Cleveland Museum of Art, and Art Institute of Chicago, "Mark Tobey," 1962–63; Missouri, City Art Museum of St. Louis, Bicentennial, "200 Years of American Painting," 1964; The Cleveland Museum of Art, 1965; National Gallery of Canada, Montreal World's Fair, "Man and His World," 1967; Dallas Museum of Fine Arts, "Mark Tobey Retrospective," 1968

59. PORTRAIT OF
MRS. A. H. HOOKER*
Pastel. 25 x 16⅞ in.
Date: 1951.
Signed and dated lower left: Tobey '53
Collection: Mrs. A. H. Hooker

Lent by Mr. and Mrs. David E. Wagoner, Seattle, 1970
Exhibitions: San Francisco, California Palace of the Legion of Honor and circulated in America, "Mark Tobey Retrospective," 1951; Seattle Art Museum, "Mark Tobey in Northwest Collections," 1959

60. ORPHEUS
Gouache on paper. 18⅝ x 25⅜ in.
Signed and dated upper left: Tobey 52
Collection: Willard Gallery, New York
Gift of Mr. and Mrs. Corydon Wagner, 1955
Exhibitions: Seattle Art Museum and circulated in western America, "Mark Tobey in Northwest Collections," 1959–60; The Cleveland Museum of Art, "Paths of Abstract Art," 1960; Paris, Musée des Arts Décoratifs, "Mark Tobey," 1961; London, Whitechapel Gallery, "Mark Tobey," 1962; Tacoma, Wash., University of Puget Sound, "Northwest Art," 1963

61. FESTIVAL
Tempera and oil on cardboard. 39½ x 29½ in.
Signed and dated lower right: Tobey 53
Gift of Mr. and Mrs. Bagley Wright, 1962
Exhibitions: Washington, D.C., United States Information Agency for circulation in Europe, "Eight American Artists," 1957-58; New York, Museum of Modern Art, "Documenta II," 1959; Seattle World's Fair, Fine Arts Pavilion, "Seattle Art Museum Mark Tobey Exhibition," 1962; Portland, Ore., Art Museum, Collection of Mr. and Mrs. Bagley Wright, "20th Century American and European Paintings and Sculpture," 1964

62. GOLDEN MOUNTAINS
Gouache on masonite. 39¼ x 18¼ in.
Signed and dated lower right: Tobey '53
Collection: Purchased from the artist
Eugene Fuller Memorial Collection, 1953
Exhibitions: Seattle, "39th Annual Exhibition of

Northwest Artists," 1953; Houston, Tex., Contemporary Arts Association, "Marin, Tobey, Graves," 1956; Washington, D.C., United States Information Agency for circulation in Asia and Australia, "Eight American Artists," 1957–58; New York, The American Federation of Arts for circulation in eastern America, "Crosscurrents," 1958–59; Atlanta Art Association, "Landscape into Art," 1962; Seattle World's Fair, Fine Arts Pavilion, "Seattle Art Museum Mark Tobey Exhibition," 1962; Bellingham, Wash., The Whatcom Museum of History and Art, "Green Gold Harvest," 1969

63. UNTITLED CALLIGRAPHIC
Tempera. 37⅛ x 11 in.
Signed and dated lower right: Tobey '53
Collection: Purchased from the artist
Gift of Miss Joanna Eckstein, 1970
Exhibition: Seattle Art Museum, "Mark Tobey in Northwest Collections," 1959

64. CANALS
Gouache on paper. 17¾ x 11⅞ in.
Signed and dated lower right: Tobey '54
Collection: Seligman Gallery, Seattle
Eugene Fuller Memorial Collection, 1954
Exhibitions: Seattle, Seligman Gallery, "Mark Tobey," 1954; San Francisco Museum of Art and circulated in America, "Pacific Coast Art," 1956–57; Venice, "XXIX Biennale Venezia," 1958; Seattle Art Museum and circulated in western America, "Mark Tobey in Northwest Collections," 1959–60; Seattle World's Fair, Fine Arts Pavilion, "Seattle Art Museum Mark Tobey Exhibition," 1962

65. CHOIR II
Gouache on paper. 16½ x 10 in.
Signed and dated lower right: Tobey '54
Collection: Seligman Gallery, Seattle
Eugene Fuller Memorial Collection, 1955
Exhibitions: Seattle, Seligman Gallery, "Mark

Tobey," 1954; Houston, Tex., Contemporary Arts Association, "Marin, Tobey, Graves," 1956; Tucson Art Center, "Pacific Coast Painting," 1957; Tacoma Art League, "Christmas Exhibition," 1958; Seattle Art Museum and circulated in western America, "Mark Tobey in Northwest Collections," 1959–60; Seattle World's Fair, Fine Arts Pavilion, "Seattle Art Museum Mark Tobey Exhibition," 1962; Tacoma, Wash., University of Puget Sound, "Northwest Art," 1969

66. JAPANESE FANTASY
Gouache on paper. 17⅞ x 11¾ in.
Signed and dated lower right: Tobey '54
Collection: Willard Gallery, New York
Eugene Fuller Memorial Collection, 1956
Exhibitions: New York, Willard Gallery, "Mark Tobey," 1956; Seattle Art Museum, "Mark Tobey in Northwest Collections," 1959; The Cleveland Museum of Art, "Paths of Abstract Art," 1960; Seattle World's Fair, Fine Arts Pavilion, "Seattle Art Museum Mark Tobey Exhibition," 1962; Seattle Center, International Pavilion, 1963; Spokane, Wash., Cheney Cowles Memorial Museum, "Mark Tobey Retrospective," 1968

67. SERPENTINE
Gouache and pencil on paper. 29¾ x 39½ in.
Signed and dated lower right: Tobey 55
Collection: Willard Gallery, New York
Purchased through Seattle Art Museum's Silver Anniversary Fund, 1958
Exhibitions: Washington, D.C., United States Information Agency for circulation in Europe, "Eight American Artists," 1957–58; New York, Willard Gallery, "Mark Tobey," 1958; Seattle Art Museum, "Mark Tobey in Northwest Collections," 1959; Seattle World's Fair and Boston, Institute of Contemporary Art, "Art since 1950," 1962; New York, Museum of Modern Art and circulated in America, "The U.S. Government Art Projects: Some Distinguished Alumni,"

1963–64; New York, The American Federation of Arts for circulation in America and Canada, "American Painting: The 1950's," 1968

68. HEAD*
Sumi. 20⅞ x 14⅝ in.
Signed and dated lower right: Tobey '57
Collection: Mr. and Mrs. C. Ron Johnsone
Lent by Mr. and Mrs. Jay O. Glerum, Jr., Seattle, 1970
Exhibitions: Seattle Art Museum and circulated in western America, "Mark Tobey in Northwest Collections," 1959–60; Paris, Musée des Arts Décoratifs, "Mark Tobey," 1961; New York, Museum of Modern Art, The Cleveland Museum of Art, and Art Institute of Chicago, "Mark Tobey," 1962–63; Amsterdam, Stedelijk Museum and circulated in Europe, "Mark Tobey," 1966

69. JUNE NIGHT
Gouache on paper. 11⅜ x 17⅞ in.
Signed and dated lower right: Tobey 57
Collection: Otto Seligman Gallery, Seattle
Eugene Fuller Memorial Collection, 1957
Exhibitions: Seattle, Otto Seligman Gallery, "Mark Tobey," 1957; Washington, D.C., Smithsonian Institution for circulation in America and Canada, "Northwest Painters Today," 1959–60; Dallas Museum of Fine Arts, "Mark Tobey Retrospective," 1968

70. SPACE RITUAL NO. 1
Sumi. 21½ x 29¾ in.
Signed and dated lower right: Tobey 57
Collection: Willard Gallery, New York
Eugene Fuller Memorial Collection, 1959
Exhibitions: New York, Willard Gallery, "Mark Tobey," 1959; Seattle Art Museum, "Mark Tobey in Northwest Collections," 1959; Seattle World's Fair, Fine Arts Pavilion, "Seattle Art Museum Mark Tobey Exhibition," 1962; Spokane, Wash., Cheney Cowles Memorial Mu-

seum, "Mark Tobey Retrospective," 1968; Seattle, The Bon Marche, "Mark Tobey Paintings from Private Northwest Collectors," 1969

71. UNTITLED
Tempera on paper. 5⅞ x 5⅞ in.
Signed and dated lower right: Tobey 57
Gift of Mrs. Sidney Gerber and the late Mr. Gerber, 1965

72. UNTITLED
Tempera on paper. 9½ x 5½ in.
Signed lower right: Tobey. Date: 1959
Gift of Mrs. Sidney Gerber and the late Mr. Gerber, 1965
Exhibition: Olympia, Wash., State Capitol Museum, "Governor's Festival of Arts," 1968

73. WHITE TABLET*
Tempera. 23 x 17¾ in.
Signed and dated lower right: Tobey 59
Lent by Mr. and Mrs. Sheffield Phelps, Seattle, 1970
Exhibitions: Seattle Art Museum and circulated in western America, "Mark Tobey in Northwest Collections," 1959-60; Switzerland, Galerie Beyeler, "Arp, Bissier, Nicholson, Tobey," 1963; Seattle, The Bon Marche, "Mark Tobey Paintings from Private Northwest Collectors," 1969

74. WRITTEN OVER THE PLAINS NO. 2
Tempera on paper. 12½ x 9¾ in.
Signed and dated lower right: Tobey 59
Gift of the artist and Otto Seligman Gallery, 1959
Exhibitions: Seattle World's Fair, Fine Arts Pavilion, "Seattle Art Museum Mark Tobey Exhibition," 1952; Tacoma, Wash., University of Puget Sound, "Northwest Art," 1963; Los Angeles, Municipal Art Commission's Arrangement for exhibition at Amerika Haus, Berlin, "Pacific Heritage," 1965; Seattle, Western Association of

Art Museums for circulation in Kobe, Japan, and western America, "Seattle to Kobe Exhibition: 35 Seattle Artists," 1966–67; Spokane, Wash., Cheney Cowles Memorial Museum, "Mark Tobey Retrospective," 1968; Halifax, Canada, Nova Scotia Museum of Fine Arts, "Painters of the Northwest School," 1969

75. SPRING RHYTHMS
Tempera and glue. 9½ x 8⅜ in.
Signed and dated lower right: Tobey 61
Collection: Otto Seligman Gallery, Seattle
Gift of Dr. and Mrs. Richard E. Fuller, 1970
Exhibitions: Seattle, Otto Seligman Gallery, "Mark Tobey," 1961; Washington, D.C., Gallery of Modern Art and Seattle Art Museum, in collaboration with Contemporary Art Council (Seattle Art Museum), "Twentieth Century Painting from Collections in the State of Washington," 1966

76. LES SIGNES*
Tempera. 38½ x 27 in.
Signed and dated lower left: Tobey 62
Collection: Mark Tobey
Lent by Francine Seders Gallery, Seattle, 1970
Exhibitions: Seattle World's Fair, Fine Arts Pavilion, "Seattle Art Museum Mark Tobey Exhibition," 1962; Amsterdam, Stedelijk Museum and circulated in Europe, "Mark Tobey," 1966–67; Dallas Museum of Fine Arts, "Mark Tobey Retrospective," 1968; Seattle, The Bon Marche, "Mark Tobey Paintings from Private Northwest Collectors," 1969

77. PARNASSUS*
Oil on canvas. 84½ x 50 in.
Signed: Tobey. Date: 1963
Lent by Virginia Wright Fund
Exhibitions: Ballbridge, Ireland, "Rosc" ("Poetry of Vision"), 1967; Osaka, Japan, Expo '70, Washington State Pavilion, 1970

78. URBAN RENEWAL
Color lithograph on Bassingwerk parchment. 10⅞ x 8⅜ in.
Signed and dated lower right: Tobey 64
Produced to accompany limited boxed and autographed edition (100 copies) of *Mark Tobey: The World of a Market* (Seattle: University of Washington Press, 1964)
Collection: University of Washington Press, gift to Dr. Richard E. Fuller; Eugene Fuller Memorial Collection, 1970

79. GARDEN
Tempera on illustration board. 22½ x 17¼ in.
Signed and dated lower right: Tobey 65
Collection: Otto Seligman Gallery, Seattle
Eugene Fuller Memorial Collection, 1966
Exhibitions: Seattle, Otto Seligman Gallery, "Mark Tobey," 1966; Olympia, Wash., State Capitol Museum, "Mark Tobey Exhibition," 1966; Colorado Springs Fine Arts Center, "New Accessions U.S.A.," 1966; Spokane, Wash., Cheney Cowles Memorial Museum, "Mark Tobey Retrospective," 1968; Cleveland Institute of Art, "A View of Contemporary American Watercolor," 1968; Tacoma, Wash., University of Puget Sound, "Northwest Art," 1969

80. SIGNS AND MESSENGERS
Tempera on board. 39¾ x 28⅜ in.
Signed and dated lower right: Tobey '67
Collection: Willard Gallery, New York
Eugene Fuller Memorial Collection, 1967
Exhibitions: New York, Willard Gallery, "Mark Tobey," 1967; Dallas Museum of Fine Arts, "Mark Tobey Retrospective," 1968; Colorado Springs Fine Arts Center, "New Accessions, U.S.A.," 1968; Olympia, Wash., Washington State Arts Commission, for Governor's Office, 1969; Boulder, Colo., University of Colorado, "Watermedia Painting Exhibition," 1970

3. Dancing Miners. *Oil on canvas, 1927 or earlier*

5. The Middle West. *Oil on canvas, 1929*

1. Portrait of Mrs. Edgar Ames. *Pastel on board, 1924*

2. Portrait of Paul McCool. *Conté crayon on paper, 1925*

4. Near Eastern Landscape. *Gouache on paper, 1927*

6. The Hunchback. *Transparent watercolor on paper, 1930*

7. Inca Vase. *Pencil on paper, 1930*

8. Moving Forms. *Gouache on paper, 1930*

9. Algerian Landscape. *Oil on canvas, 1931*

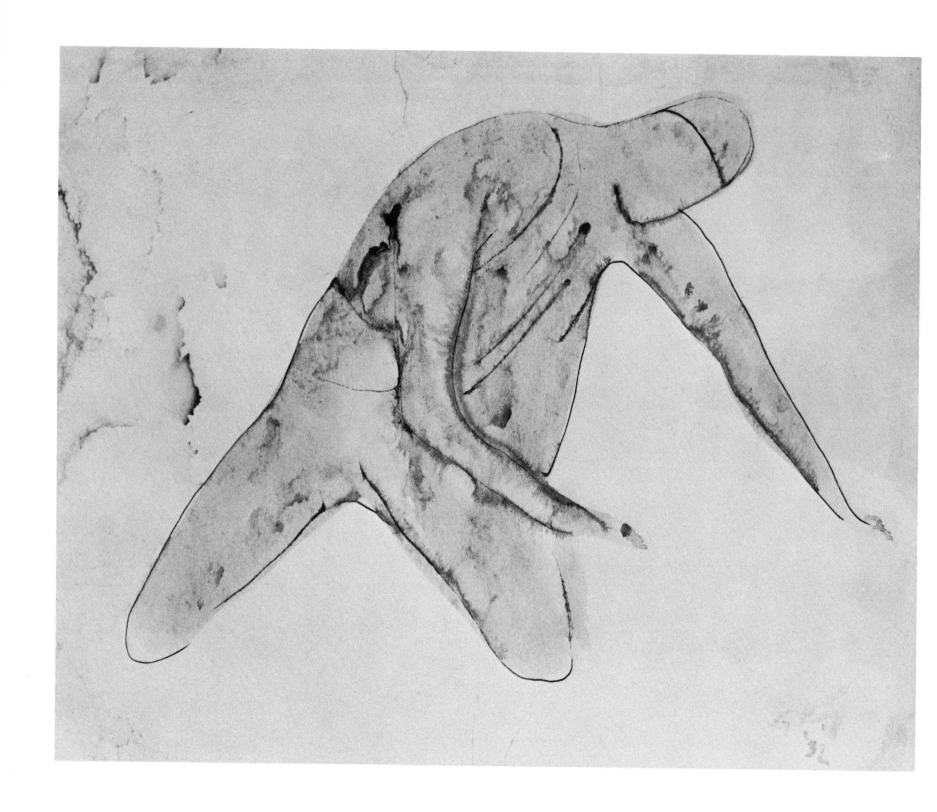

10. Figure Drawing. *Ink and wash on paper, 1932*

11. Costume Design Sketch. *Black and gray watercolor, before 1933*

12. Costume Design Sketch. *Black and gray watercolor, before 1933*

13. Costume Design Sketch. *Black and gray watercolor, before 1933*

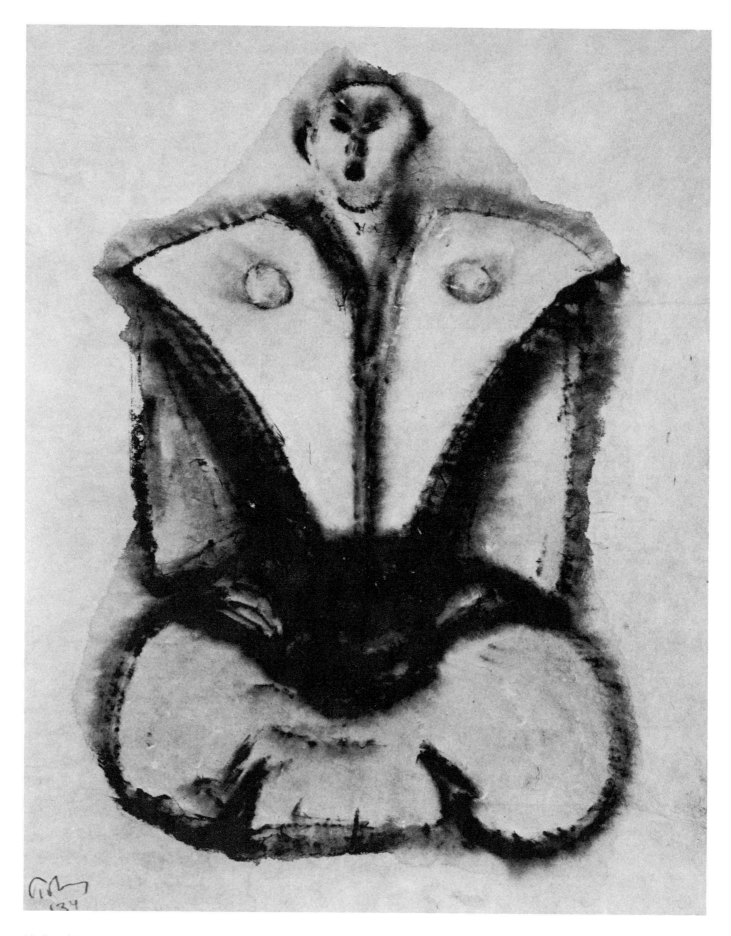

14. Seated Japanese Figure. *Ink on Japanese paper, 1934*

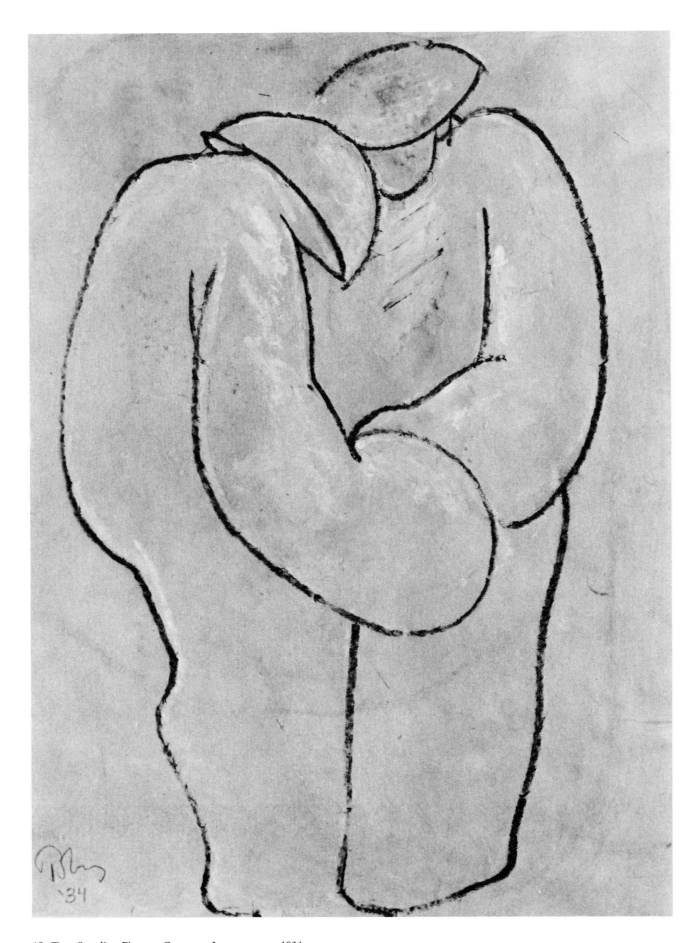

15. Two Standing Figures. *Crayon on Japanese paper, 1934*

17. Three Birds. *Gouache on paper, 1935*

18. Table and Ball. *Gouache on paper, 1936*

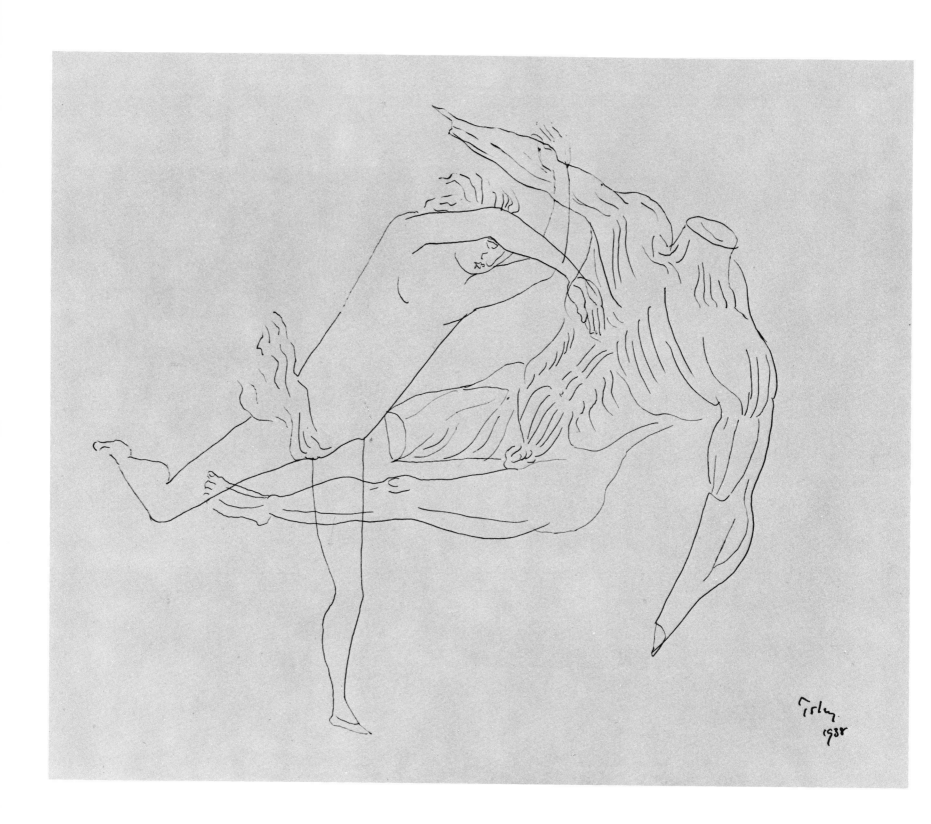

19. Running Figure and Sculptured Torso. *Pen and ink on paper, 1938*

16. Rising Orb. *Tempera over gold paint on cardboard, 1935*

20. Modal Tide. *Oil on canvas, 1940*

38. Rummage. *Gouache on fiberboard, 1941*

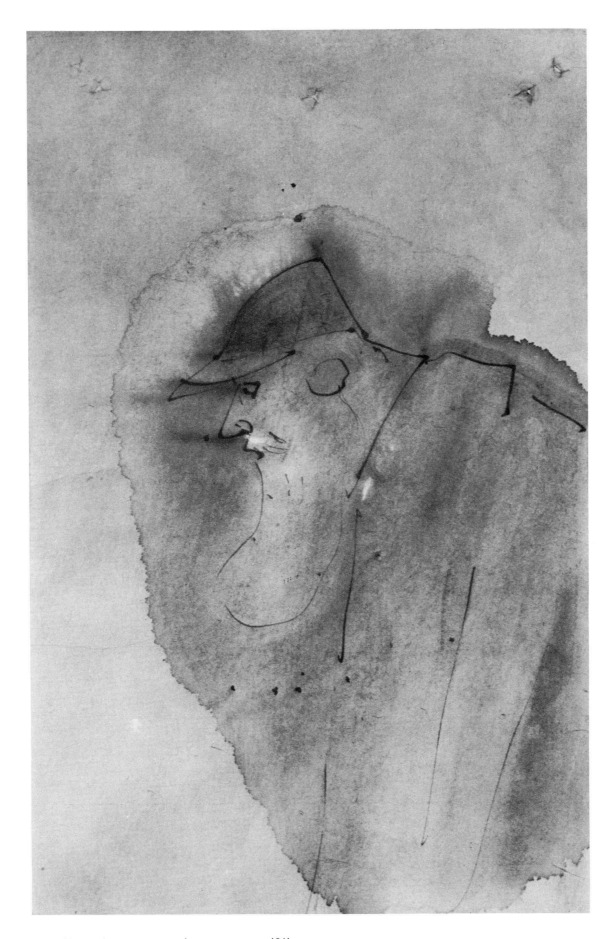

23. Public Market Type. *Pen and tempera on paper, 1941*

24. Public Market Type. *Pen and tempera on paper, 1941*

25. Public Market Type. *Pen and tempera on paper, 1941*

26. Public Market Type. *Pen and tempera on paper, 1941*

27. Public Market Type. *Pen and tempera on paper, 1941*

28. Public Market Type. *Pen and tempera on paper, 1941*

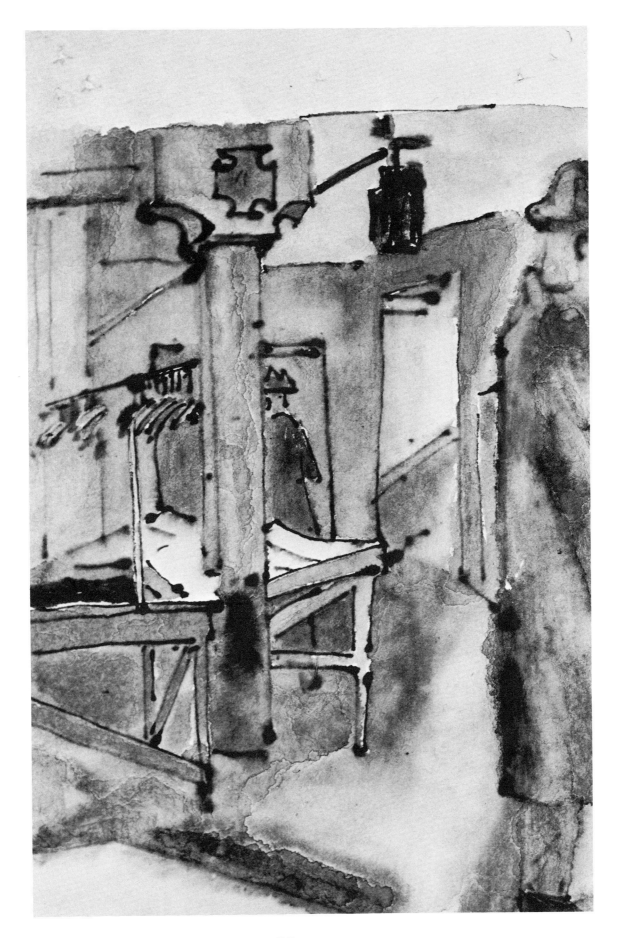

29. Public Market Types. *Pen and tempera on paper, 1941*

30. Public Market Types. *Pen and tempera on paper, 1941*

31. Public Market Types. *Pen and tempera on paper, 1941*

32. Public Market Types. *Pen and tempera on paper, 1941*

33. Public Market Types. *Pen and tempera on paper, 1941*

34. Public Market Types. *Pen and tempera on paper, 1941*

35. Public Market Types. *Pen and tempera on paper, 1941*

36. Public Market Types. *Pen and tempera on paper, 1941*

21. Farmers' Market. *Gouache on board, 1941*

41. Time Off. *Oil on board, 1941*

43. E Pluribus Unum. *Tempera on paper mounted on board, 1942*

46. Gothic. *Tempera, 1943*

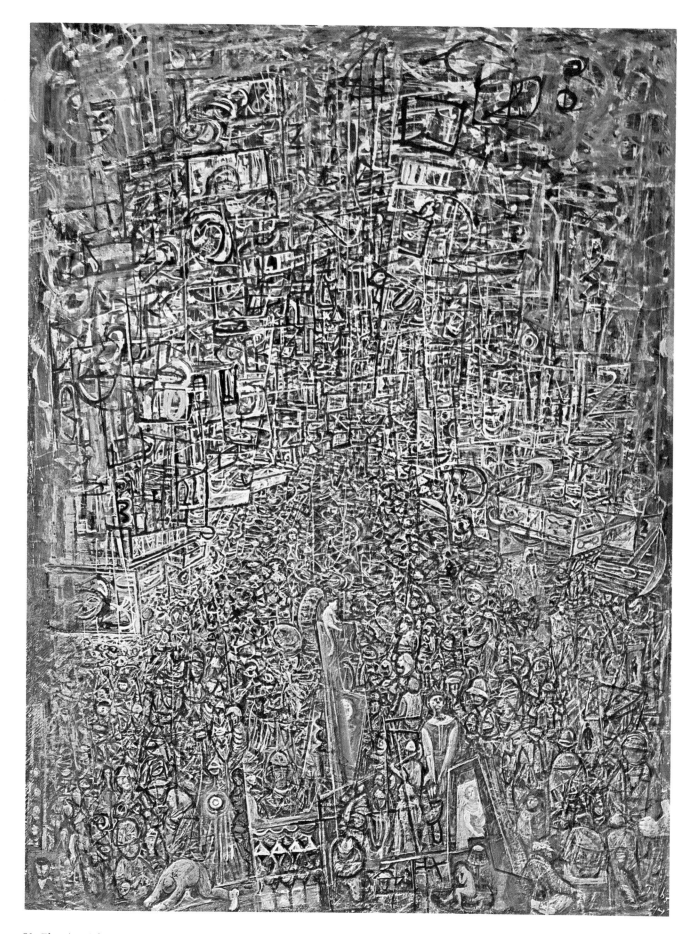

50. Electric Night. *Tempera on paper mounted on board, 1944*

22. Northwest Still Life. *Tempera on board, 1941*

39. Still Life with Egg. *Tempera, 1941*

40. Still Life with White Plane. *Gouache on board, 1941*

44. White Night. *Tempera on cardboard mounted on masonite, 1942*

48. Western Splendor. *Tempera, 1943*

45. Working Man. *Gouache on board, 1942*

47. Point Five—Vertical. *Gouache on board, 1943*

51. Agate World. *Gouache on board, 1945*

52. Dragon Rhythms. *Tempera, 1946*

54. Skid Road. *Watercolor, 1948*

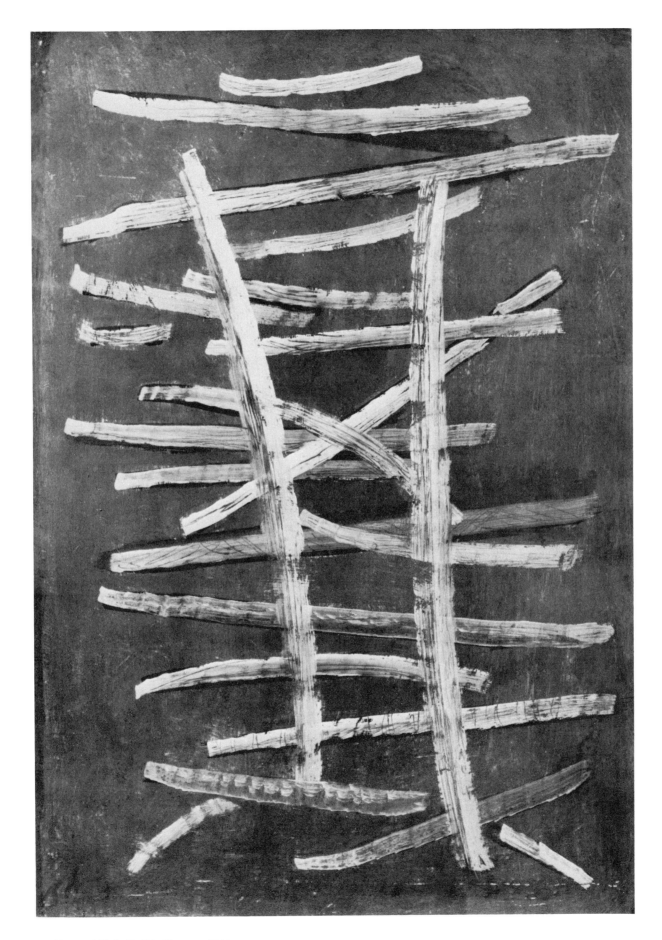

49. Bars and Flails (Rails). *Tempera, 1944*

56. Mountain Landscape. *Gouache on paper, 1950*

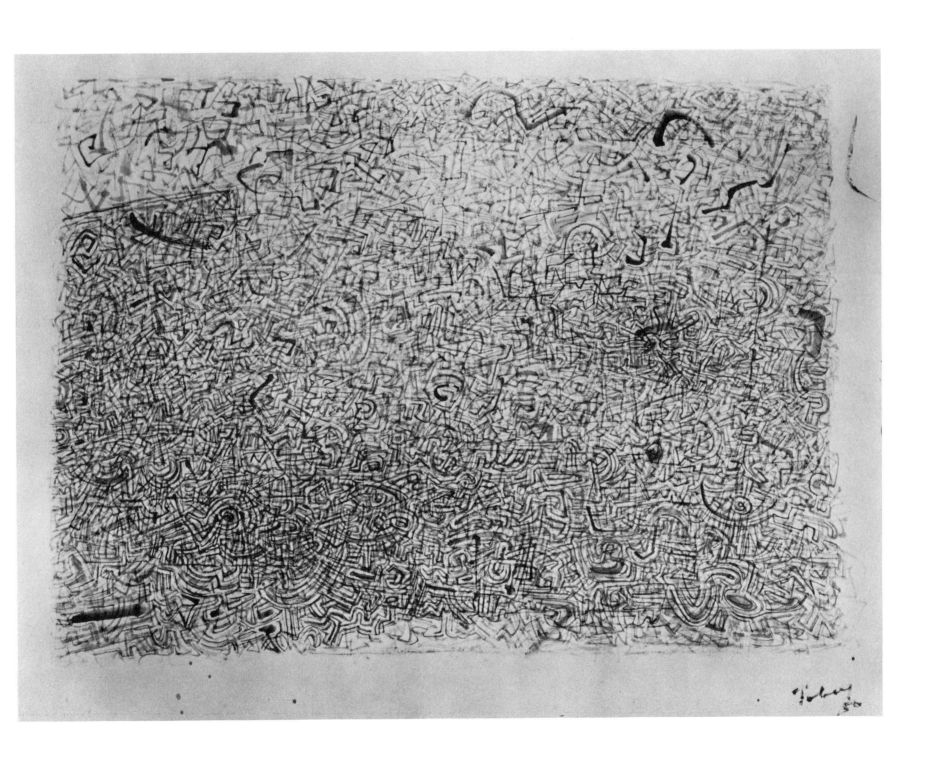

57. Pacific Cloud. *Gouache on paper, 1950*

55. Self Portrait. *Pastel on paper, 1949*

59. Portrait of Mrs. A. H. Hooker. *Pastel, 1951*

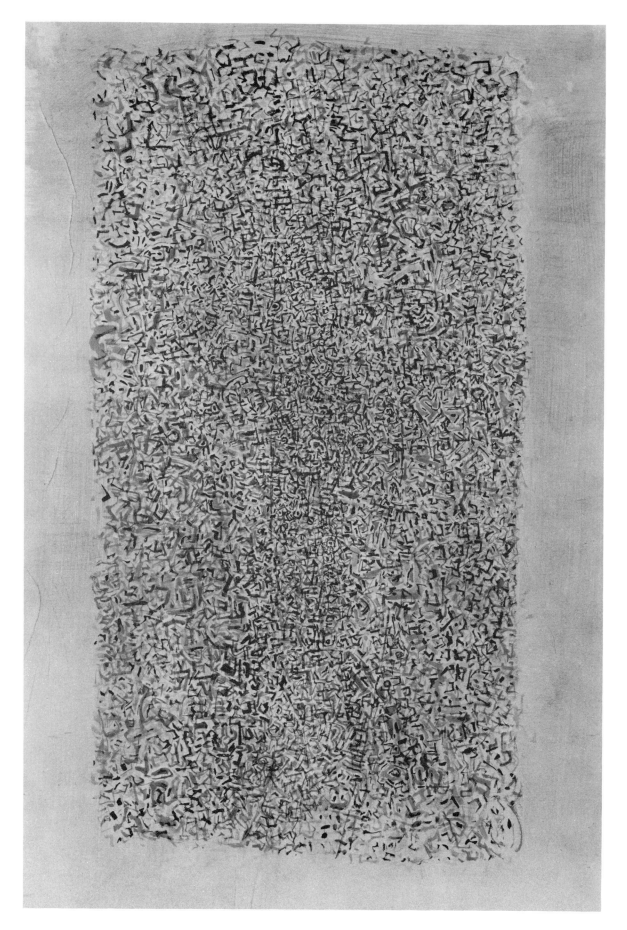

58. Universal City. *Watercolor, 1951*

53. Eskimo Idiom. *Tempera on board, 1946*

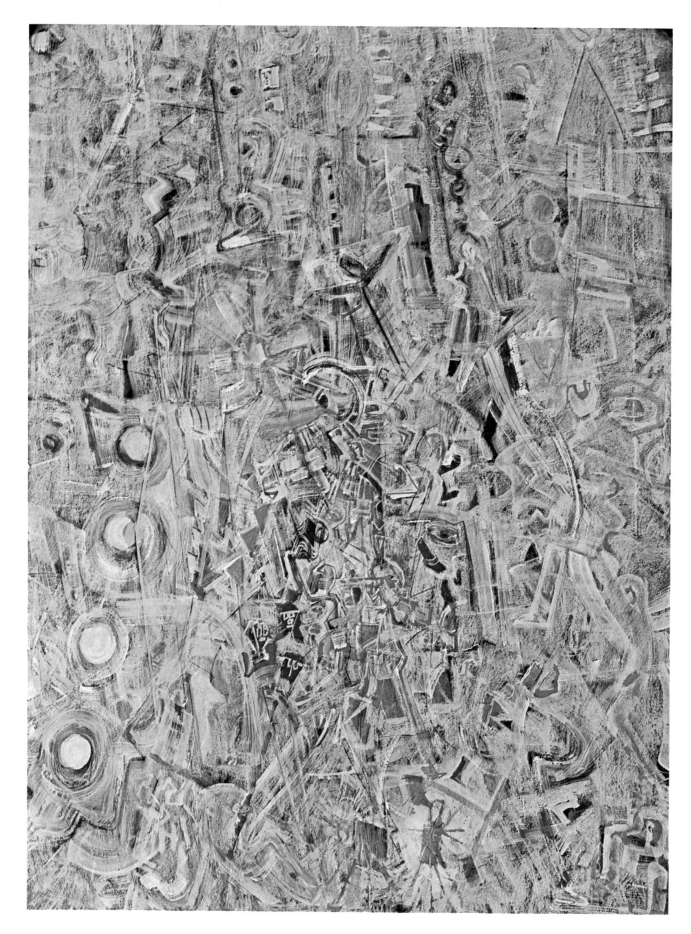

61. Festival. *Tempera and oil on cardboard, 1953*

62. Golden Mountains. *Gouache on masonite, 1953*

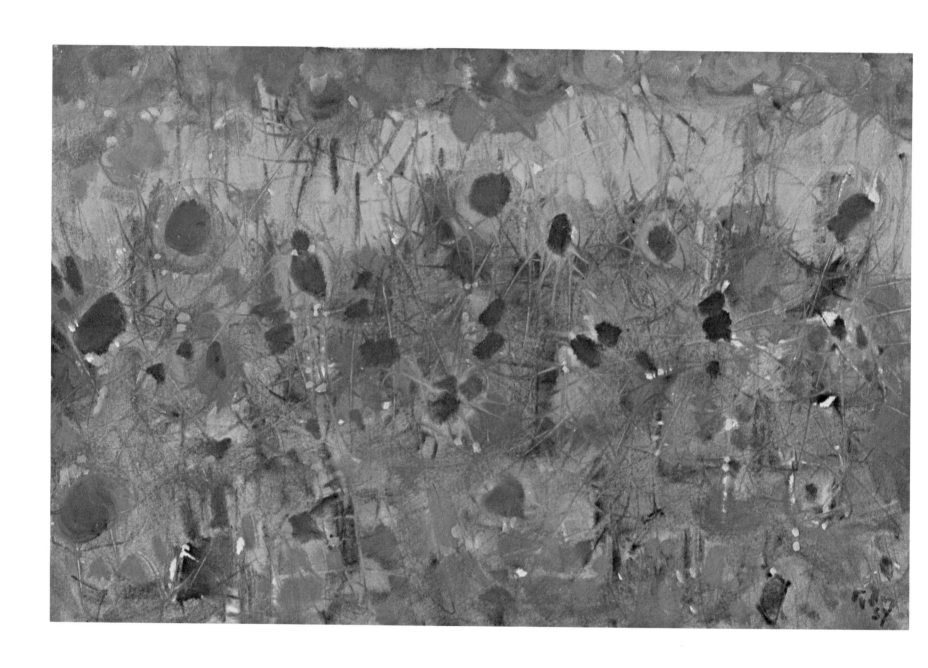

69. June Night. *Gouache on paper, 1957*

60. Orpheus. *Gouache on paper, 1952*

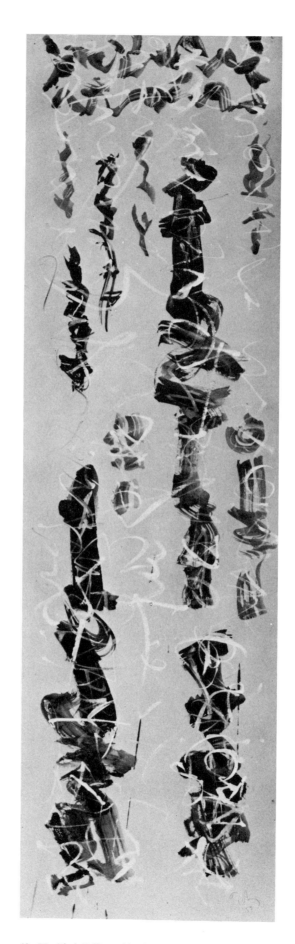

63. Untitled Calligraphic. *Tempera, 1953*

64. Canals. *Gouache on paper, 1954*

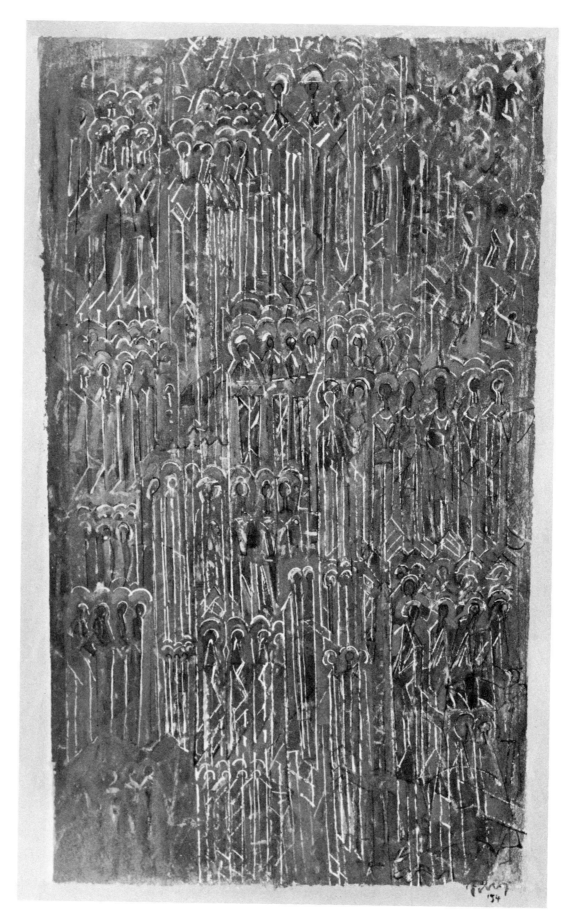

65. Choir II. *Gouache on paper, 1954*

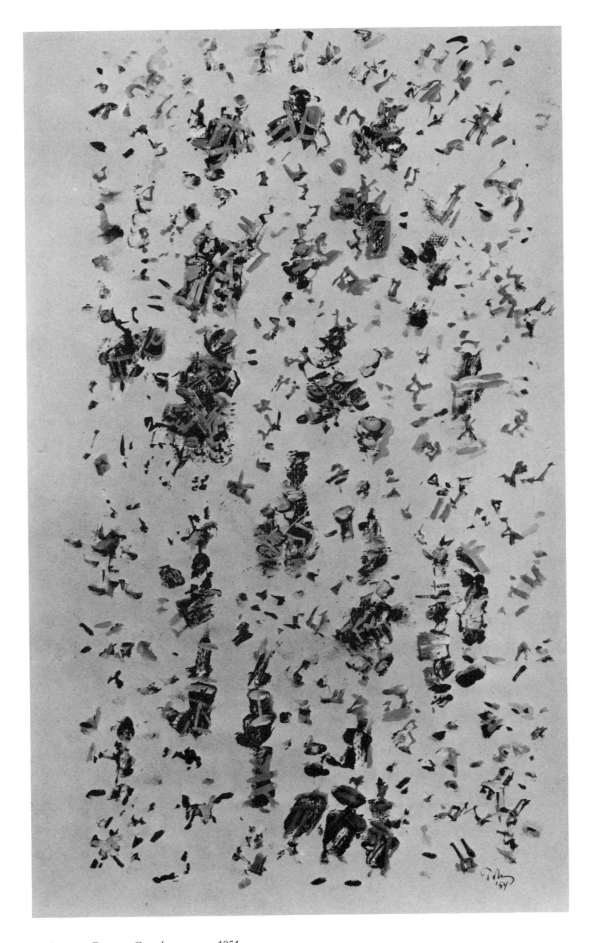

66. Japanese Fantasy. *Gouache on paper, 1954*

67. Serpentine. *Gouache and pencil on paper, 1955*

68. Head. *Sumi, 1957*

70. Space Ritual No. 1. *Sumi, 1957*

71. Untitled. *Tempera on paper, 1957*

72. Untitled. *Tempera on paper, 1959*

73. White Tablet. *Tempera, 1959*

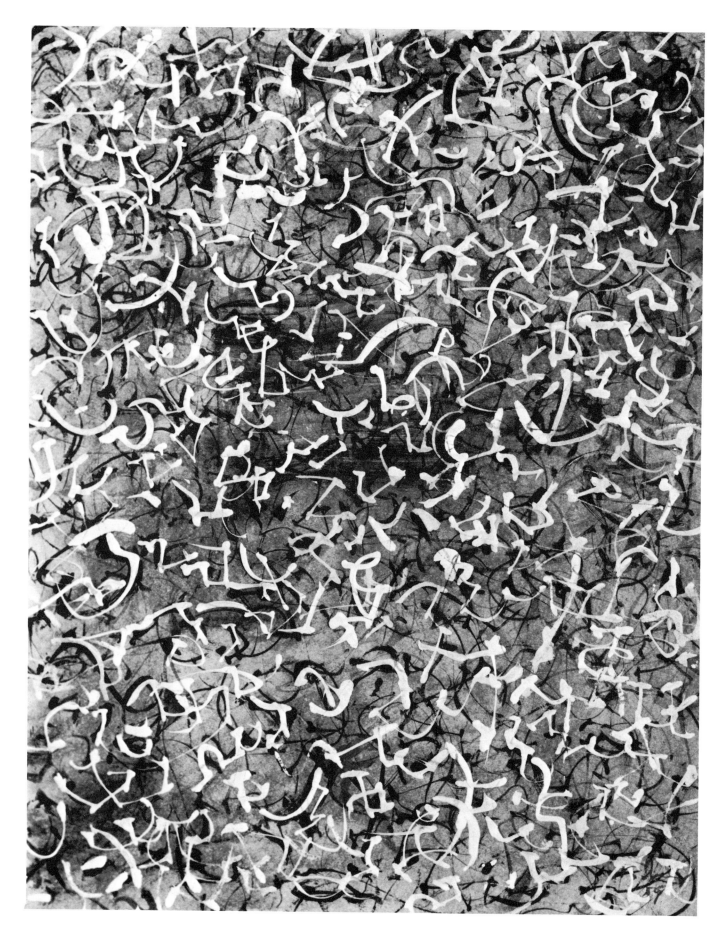

74. Written over the Plains No. 2. *Tempera on paper, 1959*

75. Spring Rhythms. *Tempera and glue, 1961*

"Urban Renewal"   Tobey 64

78. Urban Renewal. *Color lithograph on Bassingwerk parchment, 1964*

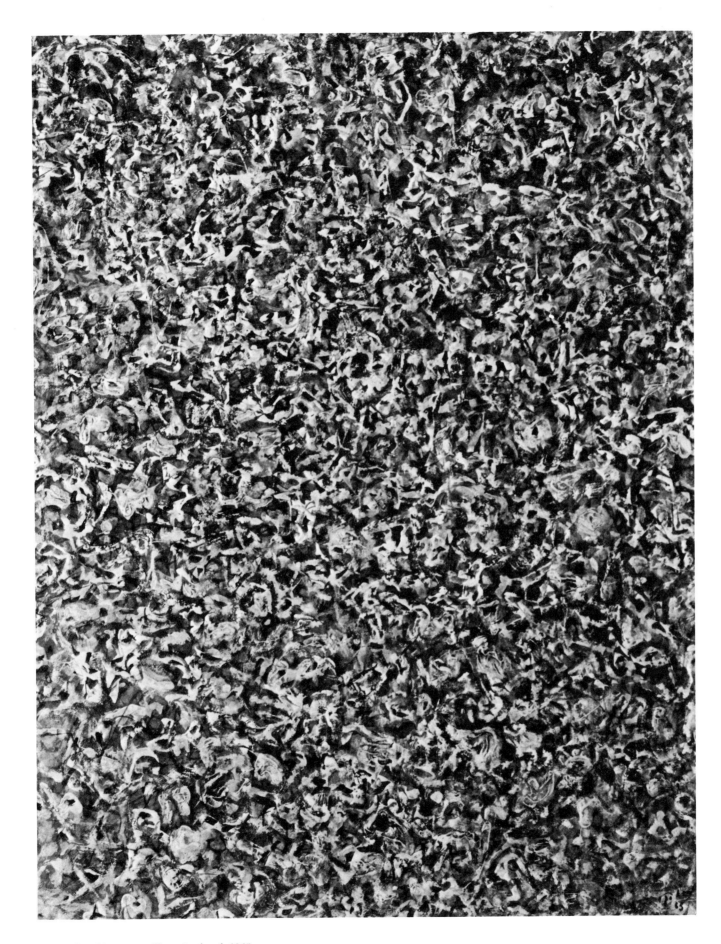

79. Garden. *Tempera on illustration board, 1965*

80. Signs and Messengers. *Tempera on board, 1967*

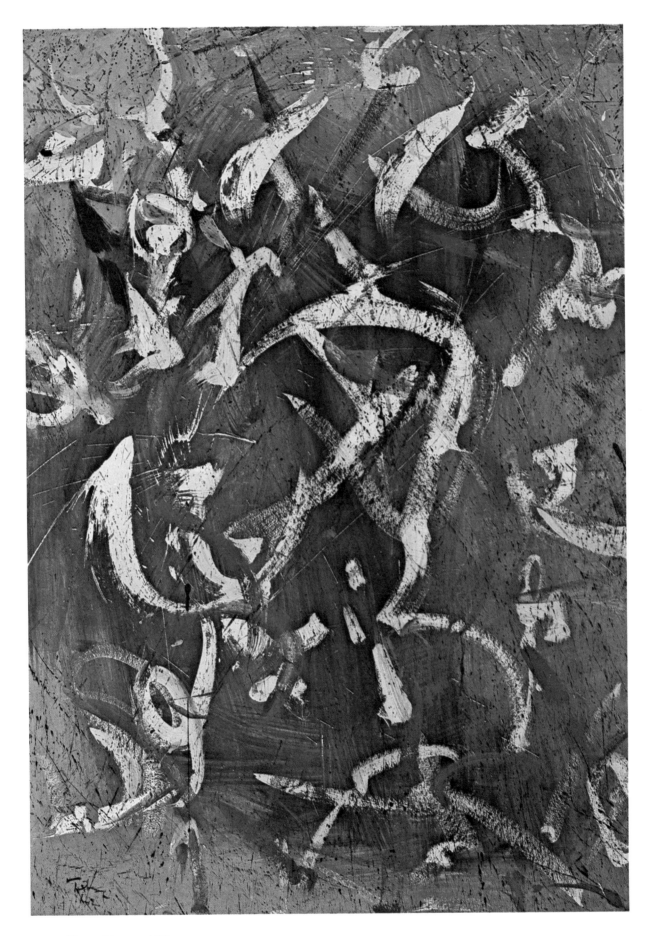

76. Les Signes. *Tempera, 1962*

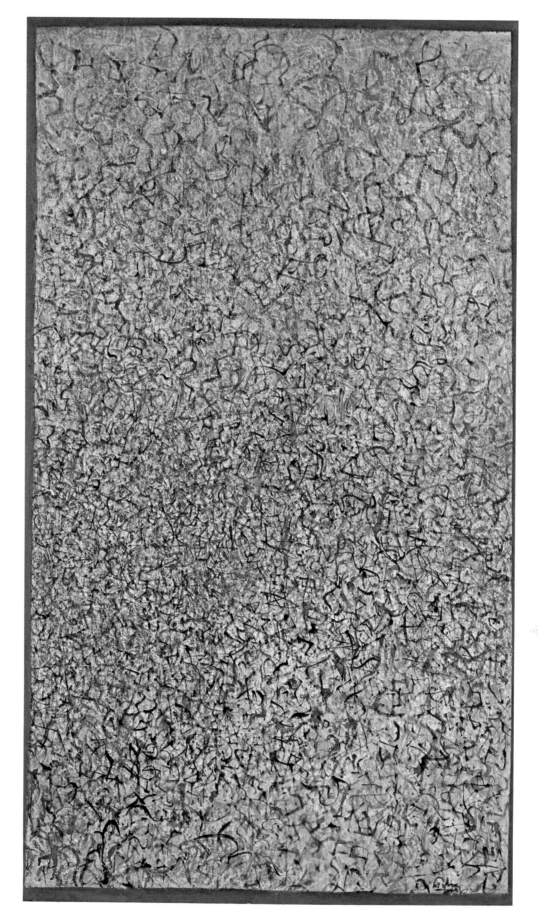

77. Parnassus. *Oil on canvas, 1963*